MOVE THE mouse & MAKE MILLIONS

A non-technical guide for growing your business online

By Matt Heinz and the HouseValues University Press

Copyright © 2007 HouseValues, Inc.
All rights reserved.

ISBN 978-1-4243-4287-7

Published by HouseValues University Press
11332 NE 122nd Way
Kirkland, WA 98034

Printed in the United States of America

TABLE OF **CONTENTS**

FOUR: **PARTICIPATE**

FIVE: **PARTICIPATE**

SIX: **LEARNING**

SEVEN: **PURE GUERILLA**

Excerpted from a January 1, 2007 blog post:

"January 1st technically isn't that different than the other 364 days of the year. But psychologically, we all think of today as an opportunity to press the "reset" button in our lives - personal and professional. It's an opportunity to chart a new course, establish new habits, set new patterns of behavior
(personal and professional) that will enrich our lives and careers.

Too often, however, New Year's Resolutions are so big and ultimately so daunting that we abandon them before January is over. Now, that doesn't mean big/daunting goals aren't valuable. But to achieve them with greater success, it's important to break them down into manageable chunks, and keep yourself accountable.

Take this blog, for example. It in and of itself is only a small part of a much larger goal I've set for myself - a resolution that at a high level is not entirely manageable or actionable. But I've been able to break that ultimate goal down to specific strategies - this blog being one.

So, I've resolved to be a more consistent blogger. I want to post at least twice a week (a vast improvement from my behavior over the past couple months). To keep myself accountable, I've put a note on my calendar twice a week
moving forward to get something up here.

Adding just two posts a week feels manageable, and setting an automatic "reminder" in my calendar twice a week helps keep me accountable.
Ultimately, I want to be a far more consistent blogger, but starting back up with just two posts a week is a good first step. Once I've established the
patterns and behavior for this first step, the next step (which is closer to my more ambitious goals) is far more manageable and actionable.

Big goals begin with baby steps. Take time this week to set those big goals for yourself, then identify the individual steps to get there."

Rome wasn't built in a day.
"Overnight success" is a myth.
Building a successful Web marketing strategy takes time.
Your path to success begins today…

Introduction

The Internet as a powerful marketing channel is a foregone conclusion now. Sure, there are still consumers in pockets of the country who are not yet visiting the Web on a regular basis. But there are those who don't watch TV, either. Or don't read the newspaper.

But the facts are this – nearly 90 percent of Americans are using the Internet in some way, shape or form. Most are using it for a variety of uses – connecting with friends, reading news, shopping for, well, everything…the list goes on and on.

Studies now show that, when Americans seek information or services, the majority turn first to the Internet.

Unfortunately, the same can't be said for the majority of American small businesses. While some have clearly embraced the Internet as a business-building channel, others have largely ignored it.

The reasons why many small businesses are still behind on taking advantage of the Interest are reasonable enough:

> **1. Not enough time:** If you run a small business, you know that time is extremely precious. It can be hard enough to separate your work life from your personal time, let alone get everything done operationally to keep your business humming along. A Web marketing strategy? It sounds good, but it's been on the back burner for a long time.

> **2. Not enough expertise:** You didn't get into business to operate a Web site, or manage search engine keywords. Whether your business is about helping people buy and sell homes, or operating a floral shop, or managing a neighborhood restaurant, your passion is with your business – not necessarily with the marketing (let alone the Web side).

> **3. Not sure where to start:** The idea of starting and maintaining a Web marketing strategy can be intimidating, even for the most organized and successful small business manager. Knowing where to start isn't always intuitive. And when there's ambiguity about how to make something successful, it's all too easy to keep that project on the back burner indefinitely.

So, if you're managing a small business and feel like you aren't taking full advantage of the Internet to build your business, you're far from alone. In fact, you're still in the majority.

But that, in part, is where your opportunity lies. The Internet is still wide open for businesses big and small to meet new clients, cultivate deeper relationships with current customers, and even conduct business directly online to fuel growth and greater profitability in your business.

So how do you get there? That's the purpose of this book.

This book is dedicated to helping small business managers and owners build and maintain a successful, profitable Web marketing strategy. Its focus is on giving you simple but effective steps to grow your business, win more clients and make more money by taking better advantage of the powerful consumer reach the Internet has to offer.

I realize your time is both precious and scarce, so to help you build this successful Internet marketing strategy, I've broken things down into daily activities. Every day, you just need to do one thing. Sometimes it involves a bit of thinking, and putting your ideas or goals on paper. Some days, I might ask you to sign up for something. Other days, I might ask you to join an online network, or add 10 past customers to an email list, or simply modify your company voicemail.

Some steps may take 30 minutes. Others will take three minutes. Some will cost a little money. Most are free.

The book is organized so that, every day, you complete another step. Each step builds upon the previous step, and takes advantage of thinking, planning or execution you have already accomplished.

If you were to read this book all at once, and think about doing it all at once, you (like me) would quickly get intimidated. The project would stay on the back burner. But take it one day at a time, and it's very manageable. Connect those steps together, and you've got yourself a new, profitable strategy!

If you get excited or particularly motivated as you work through these steps, feel free to work ahead! There's no rule stating you have to stick to one step per day. Just manage your time, don't burn yourself out before you get to the end, and have fun!

I wrote this book with small business owners in mind. Real estate agents, floral shop owners, contractors. But the content and end-game described here is perfect for a variety of audiences:

Small Business Owners: Building and managing a Web marketing strategy will be one of the best things you do this year! It will not only help you find and win new business, but will also help you keep and increase the business you already have.

Small Business Managers & Employees: Maybe getting that Web marketing strategy up and running has been on your back burner for some time. Now's the time to get it rolling! Be the hero in your business this year by building a new strategy, with little to no budget required, that significantly impacts the bottom line and success of the business!

Big Business Marketers: Although this book was written for small business, the Internet is the Internet. Every strategy, every step, every opportunity described here applies to everyone – from the Realtor down the street to Microsoft. Even if you have access to big-business resources and budgets, make sure you're doing the "little things" to fuel growth in your business as well. I think you'll find that many strategies described in this book will generate big returns, with smaller investments than you think!

Nonprofits: Of all the Web marketing steps described in this book, most of them don't cost a thing (besides your time). Make sure your dollars are going towards your cause, and not your marketing budget. Find new donors and volunteers, improve retention and repeat donations from existing constituents, spread your message to new audiences and more.

OK, enough talk. There's work to be done. New customers, more business, higher profits await you. Let's get started!

How This Book Is Organized

This book is all about building a successful, profitable Web marketing strategy one step at a time. But those steps are still organized into effective, progressive groups that will empower you to think through the right things, at the right time, and in the right sequence.

In this book you'll find seven sections.

The first four sections form the foundation of your new Web marketing strategy. They are:

1. Prepare: As in any part of your business, you need to start with a little planning. I'll walk you through how to think about your goals, your audience, what you have to offer, and how to package it effectively for the Web.

2. Publish: The foundation of your Web marketing plan will be made up of what you publish, and where. We'll walk through various publishing formats and opportunities, and you will choose what formats are right for you and your business.

3. Promote: This is where things get really exciting. Once you have a plan, a target audience, content and a place to publish (yes, you can do it!), we'll walk through very specific, easy, often-free steps to publicize what you've built. This is where you start turning your strategy into new customers, more traffic, and more business.

4. Participate: The Web today is more than just publishing and promoting. It's also about being an active member of the community. I'll walk through what that means, and how you can get involved specifically to promote and build your business.

The final three sections are organized to give you additional ideas, inspiration and best practices to further accelerate the growth of your business online.

Productivity: How do you increase your overall productivity, specifically to unlock time to devote to your new profitable Web marketing strategy moving forward? This section will give you specific tips for getting more done during the day, and working smarter, not just harder.

Learning: This book is just the start. As soon as it went to the printer, dozens of new ideas and best practices materialized that should have been included. This section will give you several suggestions for learning and optimizing your Web marketing strategy moving forward, to ensure that it's running on a full tank of gas!

Pure Guerilla: This is a collection of ideas and strategies that didn't neatly fit into the sections above, but that I couldn't in good conscious leave out of this book. Each offers a great idea to help grow your entire business, not just online.

Bringing This Book To Life

As often as possible, following a description of each step in this book, I've included an example of how that step might be fulfilled or executed. I've used a real estate agent as the example most often, so you can see how the Web strategy builds from step to step consistently for one particular business.

Real estate agents, like many small business owners, are in complete control of the success or failure of their business. As a group, real estate agents spend in excess of $11 billion dollars each year marketing themselves and their home listings. An entire industry has formed to give real estate agents the tools they need to more effectively run their business, including such industry leaders as HouseValues, ExpressCopy and Tom Ferry.

The most successful real estate agents think of themselves as the "CEO" of their small business. This philosophy is described in greater detail on the well-written AgentCEO.com blog. This means they have thought through what long-term success looks like, and they understand what they need to do each month, each week, even each day, to get there.

Building your Web marketing strategy is a microcosm of that same process. Some of the planning steps described in this book you'll need to do yourself. For some of the "publish" and "promote" steps, you'll use others to help you.

By the time you finish working through each step, you'll have built a network of people and service providers all focused on helping you win more business and make more money.

ONE: PREPARE

Step 1: Define your purpose & objectives

I know you're itching to get started, to see some action, to start driving business in the door from the Web. And I'm anxious to get you there.

But before we do that, let's take a couple days to set the foundation. Before we start doing things, we need to know that we're doing the *right* things. And that comes from knowing what success looks like, and writing a quick plan for how we will get there.

The purpose for your Web marketing strategy should be to directly support your business goals. You can start with fundamental questions like:

Why are you in business in the first place?
What value and/or service do you provide to your customers?
How do you define success in your business?
What do you want your business to look like five years from now?

The answers to these questions will largely define what you want to do on the Web as well. If, for example, you are a real estate agent, you're in the business of helping people buy and sell homes, and you have an objective of helping customers sell 50 homes this year, then your Web strategy should be built to directly support that. Your objective of selling 50 homes will define the content you publish on the Web, it will define how and where you publish that content, and will define how you work with your promotional partners to not only meet more home sellers, but help their homes get sold quicker.

But when you think about objectives for your business, you ideally should be thinking about personal objectives as well. This includes questions like:

What kind of work/life balance would you like to achieve?
How many hours do you want to work each week?
Do you want to work weekends?
Do you want to create a business you can sell down the road?
When do you want to retire? How do you want to retire?

Based on the business you're in, you may feel that some of these questions or opportunities are impossible. If you're in real estate, for example, you can't possibly get away with taking the weekends off. Can you?

Of course you can! If you make it a goal, you can do it!

Staci Dancey, a market-leading real estate agent in the Southern California market, earns an income in excess of $600,000 each year. She regularly works just four days a week – Monday through Thursday, and always takes the weekend off.

I've spoken with countless real estate agents who work just 40-45 hours per week, yet earn a high, six-figure income. They can do this because they have a plan, built on what they determined success in their business should look like.

If they can do it, why can't you?

This is exactly why setting your personal and professional goals up front are so important. If you have a clear understanding of what success looks like, and what business goals you want to achieve, you can build a business and marketing plan in support of that.

STEP ONE ACTION ITEMS:
Think about and write down your answers to the above nine questions.
Think about any other definitions of "purpose" for your business.
Look across your current business and marketing strategy to make sure your focus areas are helping you align behind and achieve these objectives.
Write down your business objectives, and post it somewhere prominent so that you review them often, to keep your business and your marketing plan focused.

Step 2: Determine your audience

Your audience is your customers. Right? Well, that's part of it. But it's not exactly that simple.

At the highest level, your audience is probably divided into two groups:
1) current customers, and 2) prospective customers. Depending on what you do, you might separate current customers into "active" customers and "past customers", and you might also have non-customer audiences to think about as well – such as government regulators, service providers, maybe even suppliers and distribution channel managers.

But at the end of the day, you likely care most about your customers (current and future).

But who are your customers? Which prospective customers do you care most about?

If you're a real estate agent, for example, do you want to work with buyers only? Or maybe sellers only?

Do you want to work specifically with first-time home buyers? Maybe real estate investors?

Or maybe you want to be a condo specialist? Or a second-home specialist?

Each of these specialties implies a distinct group of current and prospective customers, and will ultimately help you hone your marketing strategy further.

And being all things to all people isn't the answer, either. Some big companies can pull this off, but most small businesses can't. Your best path to remarkability and greater success is to focus, and be better than anyone else at serving that specific customer group.

This often means not only deciding who you are going to focus on, but also deciding who you are NOT going to focus on.

Let's go back to the real estate example again. Let's say you're an agent, and want to focus on listing homes. That means your business is going to focus on home sellers, right?

True. But what this means is that your marketing, your messages, and your brand are going to focus on the benefits of why sellers should work with you. It means you're going to focus all of your energy on delighting seller customers, and leveraging that to acquire more seller customers moving forward.

It doesn't mean that you won't help other customers. Many of those sellers are also going to buy a new home. And occasionally, a friend of theirs may need only buyer services.

I consider this "found business", and recommend you take advantage of it.

But if you make a clear decision, today, on what customer group you want to focus on, then it will significantly help in your future marketing decisions (and will make executing the remaining steps in this book a whole lot easier!).

STEP TWO ACTION ITEMS:
Make a list of the different audiences you communicate to today.
Make a separate list of the types of customers you service today.
Narrow that list to the customer groups you want to focus on moving forward.

Step 3: Set goals

Success is impossible without setting goals. Plain and simple.

It's critical that every business, no matter what size or nature, sets clear, aggressive but achievable goals to drive both focus and results.

This means two things:

1. Knowing what success looks like
2. Knowing how to get there

Many businesses do the first part very well. They set goals related to revenue growth, profitability, expansion, etc. But all too often, there's no blueprint to get there. Long-term goals feel distant, cumbersome, and intimidating unless you know exactly how you are going to get there.

Let's walk through both of these critical steps to setting goals.

First, define what success looks like. What does success look like for you this year? Next year? Five years from now

Are you driven by income? Profit? Growth? Retirement?

Is your goal related to making the most money possible, or spending the most time possible out on your boat (and NOT working)?

Get very specific about your goal. Answer questions such as:

> How much money do you want to make this year?
> How hard do you want to work?
> How much money do you want to make next year?
> What does success look like for your business five years from now?

Set goals that will make you feel successful, and also set goals that make you a little nervous. If your goals feel aggressive, you're probably on the right track.

Setting clear long-term goals is critical, but knowing how to achieve them is equally as important.

If you've set the right goal, it will be impossible to achieve without a plan. But if you break that goal down into what you need to do every quarter, every month, every week, even every day, then you've created a game plan for achieving success.

Take this book as an example. Its goal is to help you create a comprehensive Web marketing strategy for your business. Now, the idea of building and optimizing a Web marketing strategy is itself intimidating. But this book breaks it down into individual steps, each of which is entirely achievable. Do each of those steps, one at a time, and you will have a successful Web marketing strategy.

Your business is no different.

Let's take real estate agents again, and assume that an agent has a goal of making $150,000 this year.

Here are the questions that agent needs to answer:

What's my average income (commission) per sold home?

How many houses do I need to sell this year (multiplied by my average commission) to make my income goal?

How many houses do I need to sell each month to stay on track?

How many prospective customers do I need to meet each month to sell that many homes?

What do I need to do every day to generate enough inbound interest in my services as a real estate agent to meet my monthly homes sold goal?

A very well-done annual business plan for real estate agents can be found on AgentCEO.com, including a one-page worksheet to help real estate agents calculate the tactical steps required to meet their annual income goals.

Your business is no different.

Take the time today to break down your long-term goals into shorter, more achievable goals. Then start thinking about the tactics required to get there.

Those tactics will define the details of how your Web marketing strategy plays out, and how it can be most efficiently focused to help you achieve those long-term goals.

STEP THREE ACTION ITEMS:
Write down your long-term goals.
Think through the steps it will take to get there.
Start to understand what you need to do every month, every week, even every day, to achieve those long-term goals.

Step 4: Brainstorm content

We're just three steps into building your Web marketing strategy, but the hard part is done.

That's right. The hard part is setting the foundation, thinking through your fundamental business objectives and goals, and making the hard decisions about what you need to be doing in your business to be successful.

Now begins the fun part. From this step forward, we will be using the building blocks you've already set to create something truly exciting and remarkable, almost from scratch.

This starts with content. The Internet is driven by content – information and ideas that can be searched, read, played with, and experienced by your customers.

Content will drive how effective your Web site performs, and how efficient you will be at driving more people back to your Web site.

Content is highly correlated to your business objectives and audience choices. The decisions you've already made will directly lead to the type of content you need to consider for your Web site, and your broader Web marketing.

Your content decisions will also come down to the type of business you lead. Consider these questions:

> What do you sell? Do you sell products? A service?
>
> Are your products tangible (i.e. can you take a picture of them), or are they software or concept-based?
>
> Who are your customers? What do they do? What content and images do they associate with?
>
> What do your customers care about? What information are they seeking? What advice do they need?

By answering these questions, you will be able to make the right decisions about what kind of content you want to publish.

For example, let's say you own and operate a bakery. You would start by answering these questions:

> What type of baked goods do I sell? How are my baked goods unique in the marketplace? Why do my customers buy them?
>
> Who are my customers? Where do they come from? What do they like?
>
> What else do they do in their lives? How is my bakery an important part of their life?

The answer to these questions should lead you to the right decisions about content. For example:

> If your bakery specializes in organic materials, your content should focus on the value of natural foods, why they're valuable and better for you, where else to find organic goods (beyond baked items), etc.
>
> If your bakery is well-known for its cakes, you probably want to create content that focuses on celebrations – birthdays, holidays, weddings, etc. You might even consider content that celebrates how your customers celebrate – including a photo album of customers celebrating birthdays and special occasions with your cakes, etc.
>
> If your customers are busy moms and families, you probably want to create content that caters to this audience. Your Web site will feature pictures of families and children. You might offer suggestions for how to pair different baked goods with different dinner selections, or seasons of the year, or special occasions. You might even offer suggestions and recipes for helping families bake their own bread at home.

As you can tell, content can take many forms. Much of your content may be written, but it can also be in the form of photos, videos, audio presentations, and much more.

We'll get into how to start creating different formats later in this book.

But for now, start thinking through your content strategy. Think through what your business is about, who your customers are, and what kind of content might be right for them. Start developing specific content ideas now, ideally a short list of things you could very soon write about, take pictures of, or even record in audio or video format.

As we walk through more steps to bring this content to life, you'll naturally see outlets for the various content you brainstorm, both now and in the days ahead.

STEP FOUR ACTION ITEMS:
Answer the above four questions about your business & customers.
Think through what kinds of content will connect with your customers.
Begin brainstorming specific content ideas that you can execute for your business, and publish on the Web.

Step 5: Freebies!

Everybody loves free stuff, especially if it's directly tied to something we are passionate about. Freebies can be used to entice a prospective customer to take a next step, take a test drive, or learn more about your business.

Freebies can also be used to build tighter relationships with your current customers, and give those customers reason to reach out to new prospective customers on your behalf (by giving them a copy of your freebie as well).

The best part of all? Freebies don't have to cost you a thing! Sure, you can print your company's logo, or even your photo and phone number, on just about anything these days. And if you match your business objective and target customers together with the right freebie, this can be a very successful strategy.

But knowing who your customers are, and what they want, will unlock your ability to brainstorm numerous different freebies – many of which will have a high perceived value to your customers, but not cost you a dime.

For example, you're a real estate agent. You want to work with sellers, and demonstrate to prospective new customers that you have a lot to offer, are knowledgeable about the market, and can help them sell their home fast, and for the highest price.

Why not create a series of free "special reports" that prospective customers can download from your Web site, or find available across the Web? With your expertise and customer insight, you could easily create such special reports as:

> Top Five Ways to Get Top Dollar For Your Home
> Ten Home Improvement Products That Pay Off BIG When You Sell
> The Secrets To A FAST Home Sale

The list could go on and on. And the best part? Once you write up these special reports, hire a designer to make them look pretty for you, and publish them in an easy to read and downloadable PDF format, you can hand them out all day long – with no incremental cost to you!

It's the kind of content that your target customers (people who want to sell their home) will love, and each special report features your name, photo and business contact information right on it.

These kinds of freebies are perfect for the Web, because they're full of valuable information that efficiently connects with your customer, and they're easily transferred to the customer.

Other freebie ideas for other businesses could include:

Free recipe downloads from a bakery or restaurant
Beauty tips from a new salon or massage shop
A free home valuation from the local real estate agent

And don't forget coupons. Some of the best freebies organically get your customers to come back for more. For example, if you're a real estate agent, why not offer prospective customers a list of the 20 most sought-after features of homes in their neighborhood? Give them the first 10 as a freebie, and offer the other 10 (for free) when they call in or come visit your office.

Giving 10% off? Offering a free gift when they come to your retail location? Those count as freebies as well. If you understand your customer well enough, and know what motivates them, you can come up with freebie ideas all day long.

The Web is about content, but it's also about standing out from the clutter. It's about driving your audience to action. Freebies can become some of your most important content, and most valuable tools in driving more current and prospective customers from across the Web into your business.

STEP FIVE ACTION ITEMS:
Brainstorm freebie ideas for your business.
Focus on freebies that can be downloaded or delivered online.
Think additionally about coupons, and freebie offers that can be fulfilled by a phone call, a retail visit, or other customer action that requires more direct interaction with you.

Step 6: Choose your packaging

Some of us are writers, good at communicating things with words.

Others among us are better at saying things than writing them. Still others can more effectively communicate by saying those things in person, vs. saying them over the phone.

Each of us communicates differently, and for each of us a particular communication style comes naturally.

As the last step before we choose and start executing on various Web publishing strategies, think about how you best communicate. Think about how you're most comfortable communicating.

You are about to embark on an exciting, profitable adventure online. This is something that, ideally, you will spend time on for months, even years, to come.

With that kind of commitment (especially given the success awaiting you down the line), make sure you're executing in a manner that's comfortable to you, and that puts your best communication qualities forward.

Also think about how your customers best consume information. Will your customers read? Will they listen to an audio presentation? Will they look at pictures, or watch video?

Once you've compared your personal, preferred communication style and methods alongside what your customers prefer, you can make your Web publishing choices.

The next seven steps in this book will walk you through various publishing options. Feel free to skip past those that you know won't be useful for you, your business or your customers.

But at the same time you consider your current communication strengths, I strongly encourage you to step out of what you're currently comfortable with, and try something new.

For each of the seven publishing options we're about to walk through, I strongly encourage you to give each a try. Do it for a month. Most cost you nothing but a little of your time.

After a month, if you're still not comfortable with the format, or are unconvinced that your customers will ever care, you can abandon the test.

But if you don't try it, you won't know if it's effective.

STEP SIX ACTION ITEMS:
Think about your personal communication strengths.
Consider how your customers prefer to communicate.
Keep an open mind about the publishing options we're about to dive into.

TWO: PUBLISH

Step 7: Your Web Site

There are entire books and training programs on how to set up an effective Web site, and I can't possibly do the entire genre justice in a single step here. If you don't yet have a Web site set up, chances are this may be the one step in this entire book that takes you more than a day to do.

That said, getting a Web site up and going doesn't need to be complicated. Let me try and break it down into a couple steps here.

If you already have a Web site, congratulations! It's probably still worth skimming this section to make sure the fundamentals of your Web site are configured to optimally capture, engage and convert site visitors into customers.

Your Web Site Address

Your actual Web address, or URL, is arguably the most important element of your site. It's how people remember you, and it's the first thing they think of when they want to visit your site. In many cases, especially when you're promoting your Web site through offline marketing channels, it's the first impression customers have of your business.

So, choose your Web address wisely. A quick visit to GoDaddy.com can tell you exactly which Web addresses are still available. Because your Web address will be with you for quite some time, be thoughtful about the URL you choose.

Your best-case scenario is to get a Web address that matches your business name. This strategy gives your customers less to remember, and makes it really easy for customers to "guess" what your Web address is simply based on your company name.

If you can't get your company name, go with something that has a strong, long-term connection to your business. If you have a long-standing tagline for your business, you can use that. You can also use a short marketing slogan that you already use frequently in your marketing, or in your business overall.

Setting It Up

What goes on your Web site will vary by industry and individual business. Getting a very basic Web site build can be as easy as using the *Web Site Tonight* feature on GoDaddy.com. If you register your URL with GoDaddy.com, you can use *Web Site Tonight* to set up a very quick, very basic, but very professional-looking Web site in about an hour. It'll cost you just $6 dollars a month for GoDaddy to host and maintain it for you.

However, I highly recommend customizing your Web site with the features, content and freebies you've already brainstormed as necessary, interesting or required for your customers.

If you're a real estate agent, for example, a simple "brochure-ware" Web site won't suffice. Your Web site needs to have information and services that your customers need!

As an agent working with buyer or sellers, giving your customers access to all of the home listings in the MLS is a must-have. Your customers crave this kind of information, and will be thrilled that they can find it on your Web site.

You'll also want to make sure your Web site features additional information your customers will need as they consider buying or selling a home — things like informational articles, information about the area, recently-sold homes, and more.

Of course, not every Web site can be this comprehensive. In many cases, you may find that there are companies servicing your industry that will set these sites up for you. Real estate agents can get the above-described Web site pre-built for them by HouseValues, and there are many Web hosting companies within throwing distance on Google that would be more than happy to build your Web site for you.

The good ones, however, will want to know what business you're in, who your customers are, and what kind of content you want to deliver to your customers. But you already know that, don't you?

STEP SEVEN ACTION ITEMS:
Register your Web site address (try GoDaddy.com).
Build a basic Web site with *Web Site Tonight*.
Explore companies that can build your Web site based on your business, customers and content preferences.

Step 8: Are you a blogger?

Blogs blogs blogs. Everyone's talking about them. But what the heck are they?

A blog, quite simply, is just a Web site. If, for example, you were intimidated by step seven above, or simply want to get rolling with some successful Web marketing while you wait for a vendor to set up your *real* Web site, then blogging might be the way to go.

For example, check out http://www.agentceo.com. This is a HouseValues blog. But it's also a Web site. It has information about the company, lots of content written for the particular audience, links off to other information they know the audience will also find interesting, etc.

A blog includes all of the elements described above as essential for a good Web site. Blogs just tend to be much faster to build, faster to publish, and in most cases – free! By using services such as Blogger.com and WordPress. com, you can quickly set up a blog in minutes, and it won't cost you a dime.

Why blog? Here are a couple reasons:

Visibility: Your blog will be picked up by major search engines, including Google, Yahoo and MSN, as people search for things you've written about. The more you write on your blog, the more often you'll be found!

Thought Leadership: The best way to be known as the "expert" on a particular topic is to write about it! Use the content decisions you've made previously to add a ton of content to your blog, and become an instant thought leader in your market!

Accessibility: Blogs are a great way for prospective and current customers to see that your business has a personality, that there are "real people" behind it that are credible, trustworthy, and fun to do business with. Your personality can shine brightly through your blog, and it will make more people want to do business with you.

Ready to get started? You'll be blogging in just 15-20 minutes by following these easy steps:

1. Choose a Blogging Platform: I recommend Blogger.com or Wordpress. com, two excellent (and FREE) services with a ton of great features. Both sites make it very easy to blog, especially for the beginner. I would particularly recommend Blogger.com, as it is owned by Google and tends to help bloggers get noticed by Google.com search visitors.

2. Set Up Your Blog: Give your blog a name, and short description. Think about more than just using the name of your business here. Let the personality of your company (or yourself) shine through. Think about what your customers care about, what they want to read about, and make that the focus (and possibly the title) of your blog.

3. Start Writing!: The best way to start blogging is to simply start writing. Blog posts need not be any longer than a paragraph or two. Don't worry if it takes a couple weeks, or even a couple months, to catch your rhythm with your blog. You'll eventually figure out the right kind of content, the right frequency of posts, and the right tone for your particular blog.

If you're feeling adventurous, you're ready to get started right now. But if you want a little more instruction or inspiration, I'd recommend doing one (or both) of the following:

Read Up: There are plenty of books (and blogs, ironically) dedicated to the art of business blogging. For real estate agents, for example, there's a great book now published called *Realty Blogging* by Richard Nacht. It's a great primer on how real estate agents can take advantage of blogging not only to establish market leadership, but also to generate buyer and seller leads into their business. A quick search at your local library or any bookstore will find tons of other business blogging books worth reading.

Check Out Examples: Read other business blogs, particularly within your industry. Go to Technorati.com and do a search for your industry, or "buzz words" from your industry. You'll find plenty of great blogs written by similar businesses across the country. Don't be afraid to emulate things you think are done well!

Step 9: To podcast or not to podcast?

Some of us are writers. Others are better when speaking.

Even more important, our customers are often drawn to one medium or another more clearly. Some of your customers will prefer to read what you have to say. Others will want to hear you say it.

That's where podcasts can be particularly valuable. Podcasts are little more than a blog in audio format. Millions of consumers nationwide regularly listen to podcasts that publish content they're interested in. More and more consumers are taking podcasts with them to the gym, on their morning and evening commutes, and even listening right from their computer in the evening.

Getting a healthy audience for your podcast can be surprisingly easy. The folks at HouseValues decided to publish a daily podcast associated with their AgentCEO.com blog. They called the podcast the "Daily Motivator", which was literally just 2-3 minutes of content each morning pulled from the AgentCEO.com site.

Three months after starting the podcast, it was regularly being downloaded in excess of 1,000 times per day. That's a lot of listeners, all for just $8 bucks a month.

You heard right. Go to Hipcast.com, and set up your account today. Hipcast makes podcasting as easy as making a phone call.

Once your account is set up, you can literally "phone in" your podcasts. Just follow the easy instructions right on the Web site, use their toll-free phone number and your custom passcode, and you'll be recording your podcasts in minutes.

Hipcast also makes it simple to distribute your podcasts to various search engines, including Apple's powerful iTunes database. Millions of podcast users will have immediate and free access to your podcast!

What should you podcast? How often, and how long? Here are a few tips:

Podcast your Blog: Summarize things you've put on your blog right into your podcast. You'll often be reaching very different audiences with your blog and podcast, so using blog content this way will increase its influence!

Podcast new content: Do interviews with customers or industry experts. Talk about new home listings or neighborhood updates. Give your opinion on a new industry issue or debate. You can podcast literally anything! Just remember to keep your customers in mind, and follow your content strategy.

Podcast when you want: Unless you put words like "daily" or "weekly" into your podcast title, you can podcast whenever you're ready. When people "subscribe" to your podcast on iTunes and other search engines, your newest podcast will be downloaded automatically to their computer or MP3 player.

Don't forget to give your audience a call to action at the end of your podcasts! Tell them to visit your Web site, come to your store, or simply call and give feedback on what they've heard. Don't be shy about offering a special promotion or promote new products as well.

STEP NINE ACTION ITEMS:
Set up your podcast on Hipcast.com.
Choose some content.
Start podcasting!

Step 10: Do you Squidoo?

The next two steps are for the novice Web publisher, and might be worth skipping if you're new to Web marketing. Once you get your "sea legs" under you with your Web site, blog and podcast, I recommend coming back to try Squidoo and Ning. They're both great services that can extend your reach, influence and business from the Web, but are easier to execute (and faster!) once you've established yourself online elsewhere. Quite simply, Squidoo is a network of online experts. It's a network of sites built and maintained by people who know something well, and want to share that knowledge with others.

On the Squidoo network, each expert's site is called a "lens". If you're a real estate agent, for example, you might want to create a lens about your neighborhood. After all, nobody knows the neighborhood better than you! You know not only what houses are for sale, but what they're selling for, whether the market is heating up or slowing down, what new businesses are moving in, what the job market is like, where the parks are, and much more!

You are uniquely positioned to serve as a subject-matter expert for your neighborhood. And Squidoo is perfectly set up to help you share that expertise with the masses!

Your lens on Squidoo can be maintained with little effort if you're already building a blog separately. You can request Squidoo to pull content directly off of your blog, so that your lens is always updated even if you aren't visiting or maintaining it directly very often.

This is a great way to expand the reach and influence of your business without doing much incremental work.

If you're already successful in your business, you know that success is often about leverage. It's about getting the maximum amount of value from the most efficient work.

If you have a successful blog with great customer content as a foundation, it makes podcasting and leveraging Squidoo incredibly easy. What's more, you will have exponentially increased the audience you can communicate to about your business.

That means more customers hear about you, and more customers come see you!

STEP TEN ACTION ITEMS:
Get comfortable with your blog strategy first.
Set up a "lens" on Squidoo.com.
Ask Squidoo to automatically pull content from your blog.

Step 11: Start a Ning

Yes, I know, some of these services have very weird names. But ignoring them could mean passing by another important business-building opportunity online.

Ning.com is a community of communities. For the Web-savvy, it's essentially your opportunity to create and run your own online social network.

This means you can publish content, opinions and news about your business and industry, and encourage a dialogue with customers (and prospective customers) about these issues.

Think of Ning.com like a big discussion group, with you as the facilitator.

It's an enormous opportunity to hear directly from current & prospective customers, be directly involved in a dialogue where you hear what they like and don't like, and create enormous market and thought leadership for your business.

Ning.com is relatively new to the market, and doesn't have the same kind of established ROI as blogging and Squidoo already has. But the opportunity to hear from and learn from prospective and current customers on a more regular basis shouldn't be missed.

Many companies today are nervous that consumers can share so much information and opinions with each other online. They're nervous that individual consumers can now tell thousands of other consumers about their feelings about a product.

But smart companies know just how valuable these communities and online discussions can be. At a minimum, it's free market research. Ten years ago, companies paid tens of thousands of dollars to research companies to bring their customers together to hear what they think. Now, those customers are having the same conversation, with each other, right online. And we can watch.

Better yet, we can participate! Imagine the opportunity to not only hear what your customers (and prospective customers) think, but to lead the discussion. And do it right online. And do it for free.

Now you understand the power that Ning.com has, and can have for your business.

Lead a discussion with your customers, leverage the content you've brainstormed earlier and are already publishing on your Web site, blog or podcast.

Let your customers know how you feel about key issues they care about. Share with them your expertise. Accelerate your credibility, and use that momentum to draw more customers directly into your business.

The Internet is a powerful tool for companies to not only listen to customers, but be a part of that conversation. And Ning.com is a great opportunity for you to quickly, and at no cost, take advantage.

STEP ELEVEN ACTION ITEMS:
Set up a community on Ning.com.
Start a conversation, and invite your customers to participate.
Link to your Ning.com community from your Web site and blog.
Link to your Web site and blog from your Ning.com community.

Step 12: Do the Digg

In this morning's local newspaper, some stories are featured prominently on page one. Some are buried on page 15.

On tonight's local television news, some stories will be featured right away. Others will get less time, and be played further into the telecast.

Even online, at some traditional news sites, stories are ranked by editors. The stories I see in front of me are chosen by an individual, an editor who makes his or her own decision about what stories are most important, or might be most interesting to me.

But what if I could read stories that have been chosen as most valuable, or most interesting, to the most readers? What if I could visit a Web site where stories were ranked by the most votes they received from other readers?

You can, on Digg.com. And you can leverage the "power of the people" to get more attention for your own news stories as well.

Digg.com is another "social networking" site where users from across the world add stories they find interesting. Other Digg.com readers read those stories, and if they like them, they "digg" them by voting for the story. The more votes a story gets, the more prominently it is displayed on the site.

Clearly, a story that gets vote momentum is going to move up on the site, get more prominent, be read more, get more votes, and so on.

Some stories are posted on Digg.com by readers, but many are posted by publishers.

How can you use Digg.com to your advantage?

Every time you write something for your Web site, or publish something on your blog, go and post it on Digg.com as well. Some of your stories and posts may not get many votes, but others will, and this is a great way to get additional visibility for your business (and your ideas) in front of a whole new set of customers.

And you see what we're doing? You started this book with an evaluation of your business – what you do, what your goals are, what success looks like. Then by understanding who your customers are, you established content ideas that your customers would be interested in.

Now, we're taking those ideas to the masses. You're first publishing your ideas on core channels, like your Web site, blog or podcast. Now, with services such as Squidoo, Ning and Digg, you're exponentially accelerating the visibility of your ideas, reaching new audiences, and ultimately driving more customers, directly from across the Web, directly back into your business.

And we're not even close to done. Digg.com is one of the best ways of publishing your content for readers to rank and vote on it. But there are far more. As you get comfortable with these publishing tools, do your own exploring on search engines for more opportunities.

By the time this book is published, there will be new opportunities that would have been perfect for the book. It's your job to keep exploring, keep innovating, and keep finding those new opportunities that take what you've already done, what you've already written, and expand it's influence, readership and business ROI even further.

STEP TWELVE ACTION ITEMS:
Set up an account on Digg.com.
Start publishing your Web site and blog content on Digg.com as well.

Step 13: Start Your Newsletter

Many of your current and prospective customers will visit your Web site and blog often. Many won't. But that doesn't mean you'll lose touch with them.

Take your content, and put it in a newsletter! Email is an ideal medium to communicate with people you already have relationships with. It keeps you top of mind, and will generate new business on a regular basis. What's more, emails are easily transferable, meaning they'll quickly be passed along to friends & family if your content is good.

Even better, starting a newsletter doesn't mean writing new content. It just means repurposing the content you already have!

Take this newsletter, for example. You can check out a sample, and sign up directly, right at http://www.dailyvitamin.com. This newsletter is made up entirely of content already written on another blog. Each month, when HouseValues prepares a new issue of the newsletter, they simply go to the blog and choose the content they like best, then put it into the newsletter.

Sound hard? Not at all (if you have the right tools).

For your newsletter, I highly recommend a company called Constant Contact. There are many companies that will create and send newsletters for you, but for the price and impact, my money is with Constant Contact.

What's more, Constant Contact offers a 60-day risk-free trial of their service, and if your email database is between 51 and 500 recipients, you pay just $15/month.

Constant Contact offers a wide variety of email and newsletter templates to choose from, and makes it very simple to cut and paste your content and links directly into their templates.

Once you send out a newsletter, you can see how many of your recipients read the newsletter, how many clicked (and what they clicked on), and much more.

Constant Contact even creates a newsletter sign-up form for you, so you can generate even more newsletter subscribers directly from your Web site and blog.

If you already have a database of customer email addresses, then you're ready to start creating and sending newsletters today.

If you don't yet have customer email addresses, you're still closer to starting a newsletter than you think! Here are a few tips for getting more email addresses:

ASK: Simply ask every customer, every prospective customer, even suppliers and vendors, for their email address. Tell them you'd like to send them a new newsletter you're starting up. A handful may decline the offer, but most will say yes – especially if they already have a relationship with you. Ask as many people as possible. Even if they themselves aren't direct prospective customers, they may have friends and family that are!

New Customers: Every time you get a new customer, complete a transaction or service, ask for their email address. Include a sign-up form at your point of sale. Even if their first visit is simply browsing, ask for their email address to keep in touch. Again, some will say no, but more will say yes!

Giveaways: Remember those giveaways you created earlier? Offer them in exchange for an email address. Attend a local farmer's market, and do a drawing for a large prize in exchange for email addresses. Be creative!

For each of these tactics, it's important that you get the person's permission to send them email. If you're just collecting emails without permission, then you're only spamming people – no way to build a business. But if you get permission, you also get anticipation - anticipation for the information you're about to send via email, and better readership and action on that email as well.

Despite changes in email laws and consumer behavior in recent years, email can be one of your most powerful marketing and publishing channels back to consumers. Make sure you're using it to its full advantage to get a wider audience for your content, and drive more traffic back to your business.

STEP THIRTEEN ACTION ITEMS:
Set up an account with Constant Contact.
Add your current email database.
Go out and collect more permission-based email addresses!

THREE: PROMOTE

If you're taking this book one day and one step at a time, then you're two weeks into the process of building a Web marketing strategy. Congratulations for getting this far! Isn't it far easier to do this one step at a time?

If you've made it this far, here's what you've already accomplished, in less than two weeks:

Defined your business purpose & objectives
Established goals for your business
Determined your target audience
Brainstormed content & freebie ideas
Set up a Web site
Started blogging
Experimented with podcasting
Started a social network for your business
Started sharing your content with the masses
Started publishing a regular email newsletter

That's a big list for two weeks. But by taking it one step, or one day, at a time, it's entirely possible.

Taken as a whole, you've established a foundation for what success looks like, and you've established the right publishing platforms for your business online. You've created the infrastructure necessary to enable the successful, profitable Web marketing strategy that awaits you. And now, we start having fun. Now we take what you've started, what you've built, what you've begun publishing,

and we put it into overdrive. We're going to walk through a number of proven marketing strategies and tactics to energize your Web marketing, get it in front of more people across your existing
business, plus plant the seeds for significantly more inbound business from across the Web – from people who haven't met you yet, but who want to do business with you.

To this point, we've prepared and published.

Now, let's promote!

Step 14: Change your email address

It's often the very simple things that have the biggest impact. And over the years, one of the biggest traffic drivers I've seen is an email address.

Why? When people get an email from you, or anyone in your business, they will assume you also are available at the Web site attached to it. For example, if my email address is matth@housevalues.com, they will assume they can learn more about my business at www.housevalues.com. But if I'm using mattheinz@gmail.com, even though this email service is free from Google, I'm not helping people find more about my business.

This can sometimes be a scary step, especially if you've been associated with a particular email address for some time. But the sooner you make the leap to the "right" email address, the better off you'll be.

What's more, most email services today offer a "forwarding" program that makes the transfer easy. It will not only forward emails sent to the old email address to your new email address, but will also send a notification back to the sender, telling them where to best contact you moving forward.

Getting a custom email address is also easier than you think. If you register your new Web site address with GoDaddy.com, for example, your account comes with a basic email services that automatically gives you five email addresses attached to your new URL. It's a package deal that gives you a great one-two punch.

Other Web hosting companies are also dying to give you email services with your Web site, and it's often beneficial to shop around for the best deals, and the email features that best match your business.

But no matter who you work with, make sure that your email address matches your business Web address. You'll be pleasantly surprised how much business comes back to your Web site, and quickly, as a result.

STEP FOURTEEN ACTION ITEMS:
Get an email address that matches your Web address.
Set your old email address to forward, and notify senders where to find you.

Step 15: Change your email signature

Even the most basic email services offer a "signature" tool, which basically auto-populates the bottom of your email with whatever you like.

Surprisingly few people use this service, but it's an excellent way not only to give email recipients more information about how to contact you, but also tell them something about your business.

Setting email signatures up is typically quite easy, and you can learn how to do it in your current email provider by using the "help" feature.

At a minimum, your email signature should tell recipients a little more about you, and how to contact you. The most basic email signatures should look like this:

> Matt Heinz
> Senior Director, Marketing
> E: matth@housevalues.com
> P: 425-XXX-XXXX
> F: 425-XXX-XXXX
> W: http://www.housevaluesinc.com
> B: http://www.agentceo.com

With this signature, I've given five different ways to reach me – via phone, email, fax and online.

This signature is basic but helpful. It tells people who I am, and how to contact me, but doesn't describe much about what I do. It also doesn't give people a reason to immediately engage with me, to explore more, or to request more information that will lead more quickly to a transaction.

For example, what if underneath the contact information I added this:

> Sign up for our FREE newsletter!
> http://www.homeownertips.com
>
> Download a FREE copy of the new book!
> http://www.housevaluesinc.com

With these basic calls to action, I've given my email recipients something to interact with right away, something further to explore, and I've immediately given them an opportunity to engage with my company and come closer to a transaction.

Think about what these links could look like for you. Some examples include:

> For real estate agents, offer a free CMA or access to home listings
>
> Offer a free copy of one of your special reports (from your freebies list)
>
> For bakeries, offer a free cookie (downloadable coupons redeemable on their next visit)
>
> For restaurants, offer a link to a menu, or a downloadable coupon for an appetizer

Everybody should have a link in their email signature to their newsletter sign-up page. If you've already signed up with Constant Contact, that page is free and already built for you!

But whatever you decide to include in your email signature, make sure it works harder for you, and gets people more engaged in learning about your business, interacting with your business and brand online, and getting prospects much closer to a transaction with you.

STEP FIFTEEN ACTION ITEMS:
Set up an automated email signature.
Give your recipients multiple ways to contact you (online & offline).
Make sure you offer calls to action for recipients to explore more about you online.

Step 16: Empower your business cards

This may seem basic, but it's far more than just ensuring that your Web address is on your business card.

Because everybody has a Web address on their business card now. Too often, however, it blends in with the other contact information on the card. It doesn't give people a reason to visit.

What if you could change that? What if you applied the same strategies you just implemented for your email signature, right on your business card as well?

For example, don't just include your Web address. Include a link to your blog. A link to where customers can find your podcast (if you're not sure, just tell them to find it on iTunes).

Are you using the back of your business card? If so, what for? Is it simply a picture of you, or your company logo? Or could it be better served with a call to action?

What if the back of your business card offered one of the following:

> An invitation to subscribe to your email newsletter, with a link to the sign-up page
>
> An invitation to visit your blog, with a couple sample topics
>
> An offer for one of your new freebies, with a link to your Web site to redeem the offer

Simply listing a Web address on your business card is passive. Giving customers and prospects a reason to visit is *active*, and will generate far better response, traffic and business back to you!

At this point, business owners often ask me why I'm putting so much focus on Web sites and online information, especially in a medium that gives customers an equal chance to just call, or stop by the store.

The reason is simple – most people, both current and prospective customers, are more likely to take action online. They're more likely to follow a knee-jerk reaction to click on a Web link, or visit a blog, than to make a phone call. They're more likely to explore more information on their own, on their own time, as anonymously as possible, than identify themselves as more interested – at least in that moment.

Getting your customers and prospects to take an extra step online keeps them in control, but also gets them one step closer to a more intimate contact with you. The information they're exploring – information you've already built to be directly relevant to them – will lead them closer to another transaction, or a new business relationship with you.

It will also significantly increase the "touches" you get with your customers. You may not be able to measure them all as phone calls, or walk-ins, but your business will be known far more exponentially by empowering customers and prospects with access to information, insights, content and giveaways right online.

STEP SIXTEEN ACTION ITEMS:
Add a call to action to your business card.
Add links to your various online content sources (blogs, podcasts, etc.)
Make the "back" of your business card work harder.

Step 17: Open Houses

There are plenty of "old school" marketing strategies that still work exceedingly well. By adding a layer from your Web marketing strategy, you can make those efforts deliver far more and longer-lasting value to your business.

Open houses are a great example of this. Inviting customers and prospective customers to come visit you is great. Giving and receiving information that keeps them coming back again and again is better, and exceedingly easy.

When I think of open houses, I first think about real estate agents. Most real estate agents hold open houses to try and find buyers for the homes they are representing. Problem is, most visitors to an open house walk through the front door, take a very quick tour, then walk out. At the end of the day, the agent's met quite a few people – but gathered very few names, let alone email addresses, let alone sent those prospective customers off with information they can use to "come back again" in the future.

But what if, at an agent's next weekend open house, they did the following:

Put their Web site's URL in big, block letters underneath the "open house" signs both in front of the house, and the myriad signs placed within blocks of the open house

Offered a drawing for sports or theater tickets to every open house visitor who stopped by and subscribed to the agent's email newsletter (this offer would be made on site, and in all of the pre-event advertising for the open house to drive even more foot traffic)

Placed several free copies of strategic reports on the kitchen counter, making sure to offer a copy to every open house visitor

Offered each visitor a free CMA of their own home, even if they weren't thinking about selling anytime soon, just to have an excuse to contact them in the near future

Few of these strategies would take long to set up and execute, but they could exponentially increase the value of the agent's time on a Saturday afternoon in an empty house.

If you operate a retail location, these same strategies can be adjusted for you as well. Even better, you can host this open house in your existing retail location, thereby increasing the chances that visitors will transact right away. For retail, you could:

Offer free samples of new products to everyone who comes by

Advertise the open house to all store visitors at least a month in advance, ensuring that they all visit again soon in the near future

Offer free food and/or drinks (this always draws a crowd)

Offer similar giveaways (it could simply be items from your discount rack) in exchange for newsletter subscriptions

Tell customers they can download a coupon good for their next visit from your Web site

But wait a minute. If I already have customers coming into my retail shop, why would I worry about getting them to my Web site? Or getting their email? They're already here!

Yes, there's here today, but your job is to make sure they come back tomorrow. By helping even your most loyal customers develop a relationship with you through your Web site, or even your blog or podcast, you're increasing the frequency and volume of touchpoints you have with each and every customer (current and prospective). You're increasing the intimacy you have with those customers. You're building a better relationship with them – which will keep them coming back, and keep them telling their friends and family about you as well.

The best Web marketing strategies meld seamlessly together with your offline experience. When a customer sees your Web site, or reads your newsletter, it reminds them of how they feel when they work with you, or buy products from you. It makes them feel good, and reminds them to come back in, and buy more from you in the very near future.

STEP SEVENTEEN ACTION ITEMS:
Plan an open house in the near future (at least a month out).
Implement several of the above strategies to capture email addresses, and drive after-event visits to your Web site.
Get creative, and brainstorm additional Web marketing strategies for your open house that are specific to your business or industry.

Step 18: Using other local businesses

In almost every industry, your relationship with the businesses around you is extremely important. Businesses in the relative same line of business quite frequently pool their resources to increase the overall health of their businesses.

Those great ads we see regularly encouraging us to eat more eggs, drink more milk, and buy more beef? They're paid for by groups of cattle ranchers, egg producers and milk cow herders who want more of their products sold. Your local mall uses part of the tenants' rent to advertise the mall itself, driving more traffic to the businesses collectively.

Your relationships with the other businesses in your area are similarly important. If you're a retailer, think about the businesses within a 1-2 mile radius. How are you working together to drive more business to each other? More importantly, how are you helping those businesses drive more foot traffic to you?

If you operate a jewelry store, how are you working with the special-occasion restaurants in your area? If they get a high volume of birthday, anniversary and other special occasion reservations, couldn't the restaurant refer people to you when they set up their registration? Suggest your shop for that "special occasion" gift for someone special?

And if they're going to suggest your business, isn't it easier to just give that prospective customer access to your Web site?

If you operate a bath & body store, are you working with the higher-end hotels and bed & breakfasts in your area to give free samples to their guests? What if they could buy full-sized products out of the honor bar? Or in the hotel spa?

If you're a real estate agent, are the local moving companies sending business to you? The local U-Haul truck franchise? The appraisers? The contractors?

Many local contractors are contacted by homeowners to complete projects in advance of preparing a home for sale. If a contractor locally knows she's work-ing on a project for a couple that's about to sell their home, wouldn't that infor-mation be worth something to you?

What if the contractor casually mentioned your name to the homeowners, and encouraged them to check out your Web site?

Sure, those homeowners could contact you directly via phone. Or stop by your office. But consumers today do their initial research online. They want to check you out first. Once they get to know you a little better, then they'll give you a call.

That's where your Web strategy comes in. With a great Web site, and a con-sistent feel through the rest of your Web-enabled content (blogs, podcasts, content, etc.), you break down the barriers of entry for new prospective cus-tomers.

You also make it far easier for local businesses to refer you.

If you don't have one already, set up a referral program to reward these local businesses when they send you new business. If you're a retailer, give them a % of the customer's purchase. Or a flat "finder's fee".

The compensation is up to you, but think long-term about the value of that customer. With the right products & service, and the right Web strategy (including your email newsletter) that builds a solid relationship with that new (including your email newsletter) that builds a solid relationship with that new customer over time and keeps them coming back for more, the revenue you'll likely receive from the customer is much higher than you're likely used to getting today.

When you approach local businesses to participate in a program like this, some will say no. But if you don't ask, you won't ever get the "yes!" answers that are inevitable.

STEP EIGHTEEN ACTION ITEMS:
Work with local businesses to send new customers back to you.
Encourage those businesses to send customers to your Web site.
Set up a referral program to compensate local businesses for their time.

Step 19: Putting flyers to work for you!

You likely use flyers for lots of things. Advertising sales, promoting homes for sale, faxing your affiliate customers with new mortgage rates, etc.

But flyers are really a metaphor for lots of printed materials. Think about all of the printed materials you likely generate in your business already. Things like:

Promotional flyers
Coupons
Receipts
Postcard mailers
Your "open/closed" sign in the front window
Order forms
Napkins
Food packaging

Could any of these be modified with a URL? Could they direct customers back to your Web site after the sale, after they get home and unpack their purchases?

People go for walks through their neighborhood all the time, and often take flyers of homes for sale just to see pictures inside the house, and to see what the home sold for. What if that flyer promoted your Web site, offered a free

CMA, or offered an enticing freebie just for 1) visiting your Web site, or 2) sending you a quick email?

Wouldn't that make your flyer work harder for you?

If you operate a retail location, your cash register likely includes software that can print the message of your choice after the purchase summary. Include your Web address, sure. But also print a reason for them to visit. Great content, special coupons, freebies, your personalized advice on fashion, etc. Whatever is most compelling about your content, if it was built right, will drive those customers back into an experience with your business even when they return home.

And, yes, I said napkins. Driving action is sometimes about repetition. Putting your message and Web address on the napkin alone might not do the trick. But if your customer reads about your Web site on the napkin, then again on the receipt, then again in the flyer in the bag when they took their "take-out" meal to go, now they remember you – and are more likely to come visit you online very soon.

STEP NINETEEN ACTION ITEMS:
Inventory your flyers (and other printed items).
Put them to work for you with your Web site, and great offers!

Step 20: Letterhead (and related)

I've separated letterhead (and related) from the "flyer" list because I think it's worth calling out some of your "correspondence" marketing materials separately. In every business, there's a significant amount of correspondence that goes back and forth between you and customers, suppliers, vendors, wholesalers, distributors, landlords, governments and much more.

Every time you correspond, you have an opportunity to build your brand and drive more business to (and from!) your Web marketing strategy.

In this category, I place things like:

Letterhead
Envelopes
Labels (big and small)
Return labels
Invoices
Checks
Stamps

Every one of these is an opportunity to drive more people back to your business online.

If you're sending these things to customers, the link back to your business is straightforward. But why should you care about the bureaucrat renewing your business license? Or the supplier who sells you bars of soap for your retail location? Or the strip mall owner who takes your rent check each month?

Every one of them is a prospective customer. When they go home from their jobs, they're consumers like the rest of us. And they know people, too! Friends, family, parents on the sidelines of their kid's soccer games, etc.

You get the picture. You need to be marketing your business all of the time, to everybody. And oftentimes, this just means making better leverage of the tools you're already printing and sending out. Some examples:

Checks: The next time you order checks from your bank, take advantage of one of the content lines to add your Web address. If you print your checks from your computer, put your Web address in the "notes" line on the bottom left.

Stamps: Create your own, custom stamp designs at Stamps.com. You can even put a message about your business, with a URL.

Invoices: Isn't this a great place to offer a coupon from your Web site? Or a discount the next time they come in, when they mention the "secret password" printed on their latest invoice?

Return labels: Spice them up! Below your return address information, tell your audience they can "save a stamp" by subscribing to your email newsletter!

STEP TWENTY ACTION ITEMS:
Inventory the different elements of your correspondence.
Investigate and take advantage of ways to use these touch points to drive customers back to you online.

Step 21: The local newspaper(s)

We get our news from more places than ever before. But even with the proliferation of the Internet, blogs, news feeds to our cell phones, Blackberries and so much more, people still like reading the printed news.

This is particularly relevant at a local level. People like reading about what's going on locally – everything from park news, school news, Little League scores, even the latest businesses to take up shop.

If you operate a small business, especially with a very local angle, people want to do business with you. People like knowing that they're helping local businesses get and stay successful. They'll go out of their way to support you, especially if they feel like you're part of the community.

One of many ways to be part of the community (and we'll get into plenty more later in this book), is to be seen in the local news.

Oftentimes, this means the local newspaper. Not the big city newspaper, but the small-town newspaper. In my hometown of Kirkland, Washington, for example, I subscribe to the *Seattle Times*. But I also get the *Kirkland Courier*, delivered free to my mailbox each month. It's full of news and updates about local businesses.

Call the local newspaper and tell them about your business. Tell them what you do. Put them on your email newsletter list. You might be surprised when they volunteer to put a plug for your business in the "news briefs" section of the next issue.

But local news doesn't stop with the local newspaper. Think about all of the local clubs, associations, and gathering places that publish local news.

The elementary school PTA groups publish newsletters. Little league groups publish newsletters. Even some of your fellow businesses publish newsletters aimed at communicating to the local community.

Why couldn't you be featured in these local news publications as well? Find out who writes for them, who chooses the news, and give them a call. Then offer them something new and compelling to write about. It could be one of your giveaways. Or your upcoming open house. Something. Anything.

Worst case, they say they can't publish something about you. But even if they say no, that one person now knows more about you. And if they're editing a local publication, they likely have influence over others – other people they'll likely mention your business to as well.

STEP TWENTY ONE ACTION ITEMS:
Call the local newspaper.
Find out who else writes local news in your area, and call them too!

Step 22: Your voicemail

If it's been awhile since you recorded your voicemail message, you might not even remember what it says. But my guess is it says something like this:

> Hi, you've reached Matt Heinz with Acme Realty. I'm not available now, but leave me a message and I'll get back to you as soon as possible. Thanks for calling!

It's clear and concise, but all that caller can do is leave you a message – then wait for you to call back.

Clearly, they wanted something from you. They had a question, or wanted to place an order, or wanted to schedule an appointment.

But what if they could get some of that done online, at your Web site? What if you could give those callers some instant gratification?

What if your voicemail said something like this:

> Hi, this is Matt from Acme Realty. I'm currently helping another customer find the home of their dreams, but can't wait to help you too! Please leave me a short message with your number and I'll call back as soon as possible. In the meantime, please visit my Web site, at www.AcmeRealty.com, for access to all of the area's home listings and detailed neighborhood information.

It's a little longer, but it works so much harder. It gives your callers something to do right away, and gives them a reason to do it. The description of the Web site's value could easily have been replaced by an offer for a freebie online, an offer of a free newsletter, or anything else.

In fact, why not switch your voicemail around more regularly to see which message gets the best response?

Make your voicemail message work harder!

STEP TWENTY TWO ACTION ITEMS:
Change your voicemail message!
Change it frequently, to see which offer and call to action get the best response.

Step 23: When you're out of the office...

You have 20 things to do at once. Customers are calling. They're in line at the cash register. They have questions about your new product line. They want to go visit 10 houses they found on the Internet last night.

You're rarely in your office, and infrequently checking your email.

That doesn't mean response time with customers isn't exceedingly important. Responding to your customers as fast as possible through every channel – phone, email, fax and mail – is extremely important to delivering the highest-possible customer service.

But email in particular allows you to respond immediately. Nearly every email service these days offers an "out of office assistant", a tool that automatically sends a response to people who have emailed you, letting them know you're out of the office.

Most email services designed this tool for office workers, people who may be on a business trip and away from their desks for days on end.

But for most small businesses, I recommend leaving your "out of office assistant" on all of the time. This ensures that you're getting back to customers immediately every time they email you.

Now, clearly this doesn't mean you're responding specifically to their request. But because so few businesses do this, you will delight your customers merely for the act of getting something back to them immediately.

Now, just like you did for your voicemail message, imagine adding some value for your customer right back into that out-of-office email.

Imagine a customer sent you an email, and within seconds received this response:

> Thanks so much for your email!
>
> I'll be able to address your email personally as soon as possible, and no later than by the end of the day today.
>
> I appreciate your patience, and would like to offer you a special treat while you're waiting! Just visit my Web site at www.AcmeRealty.com right now, and download a coupon for a free cookie at Stan's Bakery, on me. Just tell Stan that I sent you, and the free cookie is yours!
>
> Enjoy, and I look forward to speaking with you soon!

What would *you* do if you got an email back like that? Would you be surprised? Delighted?

The offer had nothing to do with my real estate business, and everything to do with 1) getting back to the customer right away, 2) getting them to my Web site, and 3) delighting them with something unexpected and fun!

There are a thousand different ways to handle these out-of-office emails, but make sure yours are working for you!

STEP TWENTY THREE ACTION ITEMS:
Activate your email service's out of office email assistant.
Change it often, and delight your customers with something immediate –
and unexpected!

Step 24: On-hold music

You don't want to do it, but sometimes it's inevitable. And unavoidable.
A customer calls in, and has a question. You need to go look it up. Rather than

just put the receiver down, you put them on a quick hold.

What are they listening to? Elevator music? A particular radio station? How is that helping you?

Why not record on-hold music for your customers to hear? Even if they're only on hold for a few seconds, couldn't even your on-hold music work harder for you?

What would you record? Anything and everything we've already talked about! Put your own voice in your on-hold music, telling customers about all the great information they can find on your Web site, or to ask you for a special freebie when you get back on the phone with them.

Wait, I have the customer on the phone with me already. Why would I send them to a Web site?

Because people today are multi-tasking more than ever before. We're watching TV with a laptop in front of us. We're listening to the radio at work, while we both answer email and check our favorite Web sites.

The point is, when people call into your business, they're more often within arm's reach of something else – and oftentimes it's their computer.

Get a call from a customer during business hours? They're probably calling from work. With a computer right in front of them. If your on-hold music promotes a special offer available at your Web site, that customer is highly likely to go visit your Web site right away.

By the time you get back on the phone with their answer, they will have already visited your Web site, downloaded a coupon for their next visit, and signed up for your email newsletter.

Take advantage of this multi-tasking, and give your customers something to do – even while they wait for you to come back to them.

STEP TWENTY FOUR ACTION ITEMS:
Record your own on-hold music.
Promote your Web site, email newsletter, even special offers to get the customer back in front of you, and in your store, soon!

Step 25: Name tags!

Mormon missionaries always wear name tags. Very smart. Doctors used to. Too bad they don't anymore.

How often do you attend a function locally, or even a conference across the country, where you literally don't know anyone? Your job is to mingle and meet people, which is often hard enough as it is.

When attendees are wearing name tags, ideally with at least their first name but maybe with some other identifying information (where they're from, the company they work for, maybe also something like a favorite hobby or musical group), getting a conversation going is much easier.

If you're in your bakery, or in your retail store, maybe a name tag doesn't make sense. Then again, how many of your visitors today really know you?

How would you like them all to know you by your first name?

There's a level of intimacy and relationship acceleration that goes with knowing someone's first name, and telling a customer – from square one – that you want to get to know them better.

Is a name tag the best place to promote your Web site? Probably not. Your customers aren't looking at your name tag long enough to read a long Web address, and name tags themselves are often small enough that Web addresses would have to be printed in fonts that are too small to read anyway.

But I bring up name tags here not because of their value in directly promoting your Web address, but in their value in directly promoting YOU!

If a current or prospective customer feels comfortable with you, they'll be more likely to do business with you again.

And that means all of your Web marketing will work even harder.

As we've discussed previously in this book, people want to do business with other people they like. They want to help people they like.

Be someone people like. Give them a reason, right off the bat, to have a first-name-basis relationship with you.

It will make them visit your Web site, sign up for your email newsletters, and deepen their profitable relationship with you – online and offline – far more quickly.

STEP TWENTY FIVE ACTION ITEMS:
Wear a name tag (and have every employee wear one too).
Encourage your customers to call you by your first name.

Step 26: Write a press release (or two, or three…)

Ten years ago, press releases were largely irrelevant unless you could get the press to pick it up and write about it. If you couldn't get a reporter interested, you were wasting your time.

But that's all changed, thanks to the Internet. Now, getting a newspaper or other publication to write up your press release is icing on the cake. With a good press release and the right self-directed distribution channels, you can get your OWN press coverage!

Why would you want to do this? News stories are seen as typically more credible than straight advertisements. Their nature also allows you to directly promote new and exciting things going on in your business, and to over time establish a "paper trail" of such announcements so that current and prospective customers can see how active you've been.

What's more, press releases today are easily and widely circulated across the Internet. Publishing a few press releases about your business makes you far more discoverable on search engines, which will drive more visitors back to your Web site.

Never written a press release before? Doesn't matter. Here are a few steps to get you started:

> **1. What will you write about?** Sit down and make a list of things in your business over the past few months that could have been newsworthy. It could have been things like an open house, grand opening of a new store, introduction of a new product line, longer seasonal hours to accommodate more customers, etc. The list of press release topics is endless. Now think through the next few weeks and months of your business, and make a quick

timeline of the events, activities and news you might want to convert into a press release.

2. How do you write a press release? If you've never written a press release before, I highly recommend looking at other press releases for inspiration. Go to any of your favorite company's Web sites, and look for the "press area" link at the bottom of the site. You'll be able to find the company's press releases from there, and can emulate the format you think looks best. In general, you'll want to have a strong headline, a more descriptive but brief sub-headline, a strong first paragraph that describes your news, followed by 3-5 paragraphs going into more detail, including a quote or two, etc. End the press release with contact information for press to call if they have questions. Make sure you integrate your Web site address aggressively into the press release, so that readers (online and offline) know how to quickly and easily visit you online to learn more.

3. How do you make the press release official? Putting a press release on a newswire is very easy. The most efficient way to do it is through companies such as PRNewswire and BusinessWire, both of which can be easily found online. If you only want to distribute your press release in your local market, it'll cost less than $100 in most cases. Using these services gives you extra credibility, and typically extra viewership among reporters and editors. But if you want to get your release out faster, and a bit less expensively, try one of the various free online press release distribution services, such as PRWeb, free-press-release.com and more. Typically for as little as $25 dollars, they'll post your press release online for you.

4. How do you tell local press about the release? Call or email them! Most newspaper Web sites have a staff directory these days, listing the various reporters, their areas of expertise, and their contact information. Find the reporter at the local newspaper that covers your industry or business area, and introduce yourself. The best way to get long-term coverage is to build a relationship with the reporter, and not just call when you have a story to peddle. In between press releases, call the reporter with news you've heard from others in your industry, new statistics you've found that you think would be interesting, and other nuggets of news that don't directly promote your own company. These simple exchanges of ideas and news stories will give you more credibility with the reporter, and will increase the chances that he/she will write about your story when you have one.

But, let's say you aren't able to get the local reporter to write up your press release. Your press release will still have been published. How? Thanks to the Internet, simply having a press release distributed by one of the wire services mentioned here means that it's searchable all over the Web – including places such as Google News, Yahoo and much more. Even better, readers of those news stories online will see the links you've embedded back to your own Web site, and can click directly to your business.

Thanks to the Internet, you have your very own news channel direct to current and prospective customers. Take advantage of it!

STEP TWENTY SIX ACTION ITEMS:
Brainstorm a list of news stories about your business.
Research other press release formats online, and write your first press release.
Choose a release distribution service.
Build a relationship with your local newspaper reporters.
Make sure to embed your Web site address into your releases!

Step 27: Other local bloggers and Web site owners

You're not alone in your quest to drive more business from the Internet. And you're also not alone in providing great online content to a local audience.

Especially if you have a retail location or provide services to an audience in a specific geographic area (such as real estate), it's important to make sure that other local Web site operators know about your business, and can link their audience back to you.

For example, as you network with other local businesses in your area, find out which of them have their own Web sites, blogs and podcasts. Ask them what it would take to include a link to your Web site and business from their Web initiative. Many may volunteer to put one up for free. Others may ask for a link in exchange, which would be easy to do.

As you work with other local business Web sites, consider a referral program. What would you be willing to pay another local business for sending you a new customer? Would you give them a flat finders fee? A percentage of the first purchase? The more you make that referral worth the business' while, the more links and traffic they'll send you.

And then there's local bloggers. Many city governments, agencies, and even individual consumers operate blogs that simply promote goings-on in the local area. For example, in Kirkland, Washington, a husband and wifeteam operate the Kirkland Weblog. You can find it at http://kirklandweblog.com.

They write about all kinds of Kirkland news, and often feature local businesses in their blog as well. Their readership among Kirkland residents is high and growing. And they love to meet new business owners serving other Kirkland residents.

Do some online searches to find the local bloggers in your area. And, just like you did with the local reporters, call and introduce yourself. Develop a relationship with the bloggers, and think about what other information you could feed them for their blog (in addition to news about your business). It will directly increase the chances that they will regularly feature your business as well, and drive even more traffic (and customers!) back to you.

STEP TWENTY SEVEN ACTION ITEMS:
Ask other local businesses to feature you on their Web site.
Find and introduce yourself to local bloggers.

Step 28: CraigsList and online classifieds

If you're an active user of eBay, you've probably noticed over the past couple years that more and more items are listed "new" right along with the used stuff. What's more, most of those "new" items are listed by businesses, not just individual consumers.

eBay is a fantastic way to get a new audience to check out your products (and I highly recommend it, if you don't already have a means of allowing customers to buy products directly online from your own Web site). But eBay does charge a commission on items you sell.

If you want to avoid the commission, there are plenty of alternatives with lots of consumers in their own right. CraigsList is the best and brightest example. Anybody – consumers and businesses – can list items on CraigsList free of charge. No posting fee, no commission.

What's more, there are dozens of online classified sites popping up across the Web these days, many with similar "list for free" models as CraigsList.

And, although these sites focus on helping people sell used items, all of them also accept brand-new items.

If you try eBay, it offers easy access to a PayPal account, which essentially lets customers pay for their purchase (including shipping charges) directly online, with those costs directly deposited into your bank account. You get a notification when an item is sold, and then simply wrap it up and ship it to the customer. Very easy, very simple.

Online classifieds sites such as CraigsList and Oodle.com may not have payment systems, but they have traffic. They're worth testing. The next person to discover and purchase an item from you online may live just a few blocks away, and be your next loyal, in-store customer.

STEP TWENTY EIGHT ACTION ITEMS:
Spend some time visiting classified sites such as CraigsList and Oodle.
Test a couple items for sale.
Try eBay as well.

Step 29: Testimonials Galore

Whether you run a bakery, sell exercise equipment, or help people buy and sell real estate, customer testimonials are going to be among your absolute best marketing materials.

Testimonials demonstrate to new customers that they're not guinea pigs. That others have tested your products and services, and walked away satisfied. Testimonials give new customers peace of mind that they're working with someone who knows what they're doing.

Yet, surprisingly, very few businesses capture and leverage testimonials from their existing, happy customers. The first step here is to get in the habit of asking happy customers for a testimonial. Depending on how you publish online, you might ask for a short written testimonial, or you might ask them to record something over the phone. Or, if you're ambitious, capture them on video.

Think about developing a special place on your Web site or blog for testimonials. But also integrate these testimonials into several touch points of your business, both online and offline.

Several places to use testimonials include:

> On the front page of your Web site
> In promotional flyers
> On postcards and coupons
> In press releases
> In product displays

Don't be shy about asking customers for testimonials. Most will be honored that you want them to participate in this way. What's more, when you publish their testimonial in print or online form, they'll want to share that with their friends and family – which means even more people learning about your business.

STEP TWENTY NINE ACTION ITEMS:
Start collecting testimonials from your happy customers.
Publish them throughout your business.

Step 30: Picture me this...

Pictures tell a thousand words, right? Pictures have the ability to create a strong, emotional reaction with all of us, and often can communicate far more than written words are able to. Pictures can communicate different things to different people, and the right pictures in front of the right audience can be powerful drivers of action.

Most of what we're discussed so far in this book has been in the written format, and even your podcasts are likely spoken versions of the same written form.

But consider the power of images and photographs for your business.
Consider how powerful these could be not only in communicating more of what your business is about, but also in driving interested and curious consumers to learn more about your business.

The Internet has accelerated consumer interest in images, and several Web sites have started to aggregate such pictures together – bringing with them heaps of consumers.

The best example of this is a Web site called Flickr.com. It aggregates photos from consumers all over the globe, and allows site visitors to comment and vote on the photos they like the best.

Now, this site isn't a place to directly sell your products and services. But it can be a fun and free way to communicate things about your business that can't be expressed in words, or in more traditional marketing.

Some examples of how Flickr could be used for different businesses:

Real Estate: Add photos of houses you have for sale. People love looking at houses, and your photos will end up with a long string of people commenting on what they like (and don't like) about the house.

Bakery: Add photos of your original cake designs, or photos from an event you have catered. If you've invited customers in for an open house, post photos of kids eating your treats.

Pet Store: Add photos of your customers with their pets. Not only will people love looking at these pictures (especially other pet lovers), but the owners themselves will take the pictures and forward them to their own friends and family.

In each case, make sure you post the photos with a short description that includes your Web site address. That way, everyone can come back to your Web site to learn more about you and your business.

STEP THIRTY ACTION ITEMS:
Start taking and collecting pictures from across your business.
Post them on Flickr.com with descriptions and links back to your Web site.

Step 31: Tell 10 friends (then tell ten more)

Sometimes the most effective marketing strategies are also the simplest. And that's exactly why many of them are too often and unfortunately overlooked.

We've talked already about word-of-mouth in this book, but most of the examples have been enabled by more formal marketing strategies – testimonials, coupons, PR and the like.

But at its essence, word-of-mouth is simply one person talking to another, an activity that cascades and multiplies with each additional conversation. And the simplest way to start word-of-mouth is to simply talk.

Pick ten friends, and have an explicit conversation with them about your business. Tell them something interesting, something new, something remarkable that they'll want to tell their friends about as well. Some examples include:

> Stop by the store for a freebie
> I'm celebrating three years in business!
> We're giving free cookies to kids on Saturday
> I just launched a new Web site (or blog, or podcast…)
> We just received our summer product line
> We just introduced a senior discount!

Think about what's new and interesting in your business, and tell people about it. Pick ten friends, and call them today to talk about your business. Share something remarkable, something they'll want to pass along to their friends as well.

Simply talking more about your business may seem fundamental, but by the time you're halfway through those phone calls and conversations, I guarantee you'll be surprised by some of the reactions you receive, and opportunities that present themselves.

I've asked several small business owners to do this basic activity over the past few years, and here are some of the specific stories I've heard back:

> "A friend is now president of the local PTA, and invited me to come talk at the next meeting about my business."

> "My friend was delighted to hear from me, and had just spoken with a neighbor who needed major remodel work done. What an opportune phone call!"

> "My friend's hosting a wedding shower in a couple weeks, and asked me to cater it!"

Once you start doing this, you won't want to stop. Getting out and talking to people about your business – even the people you are already familiar with on an everyday basis – is a great way to generate new business. And I guarantee that those initial phone calls will result in pass-along conversations to other audiences.

Plan on doing this regularly for awhile, and you'll notice a difference quickly.

STEP THIRTY ONE ACTION ITEMS:
Call ten friends.
Talk about your business!

Step 32: Pay for the person behind you

This is a true story.

A successful real estate agent in Ontario, Canada regularly uses a toll road to get to and from her office each day. And about two years ago, she started paying the toll of the car behind her.

She simply gave the toll taker extra money and a business card, and told the toll taker to give the car behind her a copy of her business card.

The result? This agent gets an amazing 80% response rate from this activity. Four out of five car drivers call the number listed on the business card to thank her, and to ask for more about what she does.

She's directly received several home listings from this activity. And all for just a couple dollars a day.

Could you do this for your business? It's not just about paying tolls. You could:

> Pay someone's toll
> Pay for someone's latte
> Buy someone's fair admission

It'll make you feel good, just to do it. But it'll also generate significant good-will and warm feelings for your business from the recipients, who not only will likely call you (or visit your Web site) to learn more, but they'll tell their friends about it as well.

"Can you believe this lady paid for my latte today? I did some research, and she also has this cool store…I think we should check it out this weekend…"

Get creative with this one, have fun with it, and use it to drive traffic to your business and your Web site.

STEP THIRTY TWO ACTION ITEMS:
Pay for the person behind you.
Try it in a few different places.

Step 33: YouTube and related

Think of this as the "next step up" from the Flickr idea.

If your business, your products, your brand essence, or even your customers and their stories/successes can be communicated effectively in written format and in photos, they can certainly be communicated in video format as well.

Video lets you tell a more complete story, and often capture more of the emotion, passion and excitement your customers have when experiencing your products.

Many Internet experts believe that video is the future of the Web, and that the proliferation of broadband Internet connections means that more and more consumers will be watching video online as a core part of their Internet experience.

What's more, capturing and publishing video to the Web is easier than ever before.
Digital video cameras are extremely cost-effective these days, and can typically be found either in the big box stores or online for just a couple hundred bucks.

Then, by using YouTube and other online video publishing services, you can bring your videos to a whole new audience. You can even use YouTube to host videos that are linked directly on your own Web site or blog.

What might you want to video? Here are a few ideas to get you started:

> **Capture a video of your open house.** Interview customers, film customers interacting with your store and your products, sampling your food, etc. Post the

video on YouTube and send a copy to everyone who attended the open house. They'll love it, will send it to their friends and family, etc.

Film a "how-to" video. If you run a bakery, teach people how to bake a cake. Video some of your "trade secrets" for keeping the cake moist, doing the frosting just perfect, etc.

If you're a real estate agent, give your customers a video tour of the neighborhood. Film areas of interest – businesses, parks, community centers, etc. Post it on your Web site and on YouTube to help others get more familiar with the area – and why they'd want to live there.

The possibilities are endless.

Want to take it a step further? Ask your customers to film videos for you! If you're having an open house, ask customers to bring their own video cameras to film their experience. Especially if your open house has a special opportunity for kids to partake, it'll create a natural opportunity for parents to bring out their video cameras.

You could even consider doing a contest for customers to create and submit videos. Some examples could include:

Ask some of your most loyal customers to film a commercial for you. Tell them to try a 30-second commercial about your business, why they love working with you, how they use your products, etc. Every one of those videos could be posted on YouTube to promote your business.

If you're in real estate, ask customers to submit a video explaining why they love living in your community. You'll get back a treasure trove of videos not only from happy customers, but also from people showcasing (in testimonial format!) why others should come live there (by buying a house through you.)

Again, get creative with this one. The possibilities with video are numerous, exciting and extremely powerful tools to drive more awareness and interest back to your business.

STEP THIRTY THREE ACTION ITEMS:
Create and collect videos about your business and your customers.
Post them on YouTube for others to see and share.

Step 34: Google AdWords

Most of the suggestions in this book are free. They'll take some of your time, but won't cost you any money.

This step is different. It's not free. But every business – big or small, national or local – should be taking advantage of the power of Google to sponsor search terms, driving very specific audiences of interested consumers right back to your business online.

This can be a very expensive endeavor if you're not careful. Small, local businesses in particular need to be careful not to attract the wrong kind of customers. Here are a few suggestions for how to most effectively use Google AdWords to attract the right new customers to your business through your Web site.

> **1. Writing Ad Copy:** Google ads are very short and text-based. Once you set up your Google advertiser account (which you can do directly on Google.com in just a couple minutes), you'll see instructions on how to format your text ad, along with specific suggestions for how to write your copy. You literally will only have a handfull of words to use, so make them count! Think about what's unique about your business, what you have to offer, and put that in your copy. Is one of your freebies particularly compelling to new customers? Promote it in your ad copy! Don't be afraid to change your ad copy from time to time as well. If your business is seasonal, if you have more interest during the holiday seasons for example, use that in your copy as well.

> **2. Buying the Right Search Terms:** This is the most important part of the process for small businesses. If you're running a bakery, you don't want to buy search words such as "bakery" and "cookies". These words will generate inquiries from across the country, and across the globe, likely from people who have no chance of coming into your shop and buying cookies. Instead, make sure your search words are relevant and local enough for your business. If you only do business in a geographic area, make sure you're only buying search words with that geographic area in the search phrase. Get specific, and buy terms such as "Seattle bakeries" or "Kirkland homes for sale."

> **3. Using the Right Link:** Most businesses link directly to their Web site's front page, but you might not always want to do that. If your ad copy, for example, promotes a freebie, make sure your ad links directly to a page on your Web site where customers can get that freebie. If you're a real estate agent, and are promoting a free neighborhood report, link directly to the page where customers can read or download that report.

Buying ads on Google might feel overwhelming, but there's no rule stating you need to jump in with both feet right away.

Start small. Set up a Google account, write a single set of ad copy, and start with just a couple purchased search terms. Start small, get comfortable with the format and results, and start growing when you're ready.

Starting small will ensure that the new customers you're receiving are the right customers. Starting small will also ensure that the money you're spending here is generating the kind of return you expect and want.

STEP THIRTY FOUR ACTION ITEMS:
Set up a Google account, and start buying relevant search terms.
Start small, and make sure you're buying the right words for your business.

Step 35: Your friendly Chamber of Commerce

The vast majority of businesses in the United States are just like you. They're small, usually not more than 10 employees, and rely on organizations such as the Chamber to help them find new resources to grow their business, and network with other businesses.

Your local Chamber knows this. They know that the vast majority of their own membership is small, local businesses, and most chambers therefore devote a lot of their resources to helping businesses like yours grow and succeed.

You can use this focus to your advantage in a number of ways, including:

> **Network:** Attend Chamber functions to network with other businesses. It's a great opportunity to share with others what you're doing, share with them your Web site, ask for exchanges of links (as discussed earlier in the book), etc.

> **Learn:** Most Chambers offer access to a significant variety of services and resources to help local businesses improve their marketing, meet new customers, expand their business to new markets, and much more. Take advantage of these classes and resources as much as possible. Better yet, volunteer yourself and your business as an example in these classes. Offer your Web site as an example of a local small business taking advantage of the Internet to generate more business. It'll give your Web site more visibility and

traffic as a result.

Volunteer: You have far more to offer the Chamber, and other local businesses, than you realize. Just by following the steps we've already discussed in this book, you're far ahead of most businesses. Use that experience to demonstrate leadership in your local business community. Share with others what you've learned, and the best practices you've already developed. Not only will this help give your business more visibility among other businesses, but it'll increase interest and traffic in the Web marketing you've already built.

STEP THIRTY FIVE ACTION ITEMS:
Join the local Chamber of Commerce.
Use its resources.
Actively participate and volunteer to share what you've learned, and drive more traffic.
back to your business.

Step 36: Your friendly Better Business Bureau

Whereas your local Chamber of Commerce facilitates a discussion between businesses, the Better Business Bureau is focused on improving relationships between businesses and consumers.

This is an important distinction, and both organizations can be quite valuable in spreading the word about your business, and driving more people to learn about your business online.

Although your local Chamber can be a valuable learning and networking tool, I would argue that the Better Business Bureau may be a more important way of attracting attention, visibility and traffic from consumers. Why?

The Better Business Bureau talks to consumers every day. They're hearing consumer complaints, consumer raves, and all sorts of comments – and working directly with businesses to address those comments, complaints and concerns.

Even the best businesses end up with detractors – consumers that for some reason weren't happy with their experience. But oftentimes, those detractors can become your most passionate advocates and promoters. Key to this is directly addressing their concerns, and making them feel like you've taken them seriously.

The Better Business Bureau is a great channel to help accomplish this. Think of the Bureau as a clearinghouse of consumer comments and complaints. They can aggregate customer comments for you, and help you develop channels back to those customers, as well as other consumers across the Bureau's network who are looking for good companies to work with.

Here are a few steps I recommend to improve your relationship with the Better Business Bureau, and facilitate better communication with customers through them:

Introduce Yourself: Set up a briefing with the local Better Business Bureau representatives. Encourage that meeting to take place at your office, or your retail location, so the representatives see directly how you do business. Allowing the local representatives to know you personally, and see that you're genuine in your approach to customer service, will go a long ways towards not only enabling the Bureau to help handle disputes for you, but also to recommend your business to other inquiring consumers.

Keep in Touch: Contact your rep frequently, probably once every month or two, to check in and see how you might be of help. Keeping yourself top of mind is always a good thing. Put the reps on your customer communication, including any mailings or email newsletters you have. Encourage the reps to read your blog or listen to your podcasts frequently as well. The more top of mind you are, the more likely you'll get recommendations.

Respond Quickly: If you do receive a compliant from a customer through the Bureau, make response and resolution a top priority. Show the Bureau that you care deeply about the customer's satisfaction, and think about how you might go the "extra mile" to resolve and delight the customer. Remember that even unhappy, complaining customers can be made passionate advocates for your company if you treat them fairly.

STEP THIRTY SIX ACTION ITEMS:
Meet your local Better Business Bureau representatives.
Stay in touch regularly.

Step 37: Your network of service providers

By now, you're starting to understand that everyone in your network is a part of your marketing plan. Everyone you know, everyone you work with, plays a role in generating new business for you, and back to you.

The local Chamber of Commerce can promote your business for you, put a link to your new Web site in their newsletter, showcase your Web marketing strategy as an example to other local businesses. This in turn will generate more traffic, more interest and more customers back to you.

Your friends are potential customers, and their friends are potential customers too. Everyone represents a path to new Web site visitors, new newsletter subscribers, and ultimately new customers.

Even your service providers.

Who supplies products and services for your business? Who do you work with to supply your customers with what they need and expect? And how are you putting those service providers to work for you, to spread the word about your business to other people and businesses they work with?

Let's say you're in real estate. If you're a Realtor, you likely work with some or all of the following to conduct business:

Your broker
Your local printer (for flyers, for-sale signs, etc.)
Your mortgage broker partner
Your title company
Your escrow company
Inspectors
Appraisers
Home services providers (landscapers, roofers, carpeters, etc.)

I'm sure this is only a partial list. But every one of these service providers works with countless other businesses just like you, and countless other consumers.

What's more, consumers don't always approach real estate agents directly when they're in the middle of a buying or selling decision. Sometimes, they work directly with a mortgage broker first. Or they contact the appraiser first.

With that as the entry point, don't you want those service providers to recommend you as the next step in their home buying and selling decision? And isn't your Web site, or newsletter, or blog or podcast, a very easy way for those service providers to share your business with their other customers?

You're already in regular contact with these service providers as a normal course of business. But add to that communication mix a set of messages that helps those suppliers spread the word.

When you announce an open house, invite your service providers too. Have a freebie? Offer a copy to your providers. Anything you might announce to customers directly (via your Web site, your newsletter, a press release, etc.) should also be shared with your partners and service providers.

Treat them as consumers of your business, not just partners, and they'll work harder for you as well.

STEP THIRTY SEVEN ACTION ITEMS:
Inventory all of your service providers and business partners.
Treat them like consumers, and help them spread the word about your business.

Step 38: Sweepstakes & giveaways

Last but not least in our section on how to "promote" your business is the ultimate promotional opportunity.

Everybody loves to win something. Everybody loves a good contest.

And this is more than just your freebies. This can be something bigger. Something fun. Something that makes your customers feel good, just for entering.

What's more, a good sweepstakes or contest is perfect for the Web. Contests are a great way to attract people to your Web site in the first place, and share their interest and contact information with you.

For example, let's say you're a travel agent and you decide to give away a weekend getaway on your Web site. Consider these advantages:

You can promote that giveaway in all of your marketing — in-store signage, newsletters, Google ads, etc. It'll increase the # of people who visit your Web site, to learn more about you.

It's a great way to re-engage existing customers as well. Give them a reason to come visit you online again!

When people register to win, ask them for their contact information. This is a great way to keep in touch.

Offer a check-box allowing entrants to quickly and easily subscribe to your email newsletter. Sweepstakes and contests are a GREAT way to quickly and significantly increase the number of people who receive your communications, all driving more traffic and business back to you.

Not sure how to set-up a sweepstakes or contest? There are companies galore just waiting to help you. One such company is ePrize.com. They can do all the work of setting up the contest for you — including collecting entrants, fulfilling the prize, etc.

STEP THIRTY EIGHT ACTION ITEMS:
Start a sweepstakes or contest.
Collect new customer contact information and email newsletter subscribers.
Consider a company such as ePrize to do the work for you!

FOUR: PARTICIPATE

If you've made it this far, and have followed & executed most of the steps we've already walked through to develop your Web marketing strategy, congratulations! Your Web strategy is already more advanced, and more productive, than the vast majority of businesses.

You're doing things that most big companies aren't doing. And there's still more customers out there to attract to your business online.

So far, we've built the foundation of your Web strategy online, and walked through a whole bunch of proven strategies for promoting your business (online and offline) through a variety of channels.

This next section will take the idea of promotion even further, enough so that it warrants its own category. The concept of promoting your business is tradition-ally defined as a one-way street. You tell people about your business, and they react.

But the Web has evolved in a way that allows us not only to promote ourselves, but also actively initiate and engage in a conversation with our customers (and other related audiences) in a way that generates interest, engenders credibility and loyalty, and can drive a ton of new business your way.

In the next several steps, we'll talk about how to take advantage of the art of conversation – both online and offline.

We'll teach you how to not just promote your business, but participate!

Step 39: LinkedIn

The Web is now full of great networking and participation tools that help consumers stay in touch with each other, and more effectively network than ever before.

Once such networking tool is LinkedIn, available for free at www.linkedin.com.

LinkedIn is essentially an online networking tool where individuals share information about themselves, and identify others in their network.

But that's where it gets particularly exciting. LinkedIn is essentially a network of networks. It thrives on the fact that you have a network of friends and business partners, and each of your friends have their own network of associates, etc.

A quick example: Let's say you have a network of 100 friends and business associates. This includes service providers, your bank representative, other local businesses, your Chamber of Commerce representative, etc. And let's say that each of those folks also have a network of 100 friends and business associates.

Now, directly on LinkedIn, you're networked with as many as 10,000 individuals. And that's just in the first circle of associations.

LinkedIn has become a search engine for people, partners and associates. When I want to find a real estate agent, for example, I'll go to LinkedIn and search for "real estate agent" or "Realtor". The search results will tell me who in my network is also networked with a real estate agent.

And I can assume that, if a friend or associate of mine is already "linked" to that agent, then they must be a good agent.

In this way, LinkedIn operates as a virtual, online recommendation service. And this is exactly where it can be incredibly valuable to you.

You can check out my own LinkedIn profile as an example:

http://www.linkedin.com/in/mattheinz

Setting up your own LinkedIn profile is easy, fast and free. Once you're set up, simply invite others to "join" your network. LinkedIn even has pre-written invitations to make this step simple.

The bigger your network, the more people can discover you. And more people in your network can virtually recommend you to their own network.

And the more people will discover, and use, your business.

STEP THIRTY NINE ACTION ITEMS:
Open a profile on LinkedIn.
Invite your friends, partners and business associates.

Step 40: Clubs and associations

Networking and participating in local clubs and associations can be a valuable way to learn new ideas directly for your business, but also to drive more customers back to your Web site, and into your business as well.

This is more than just your local Chamber of Commerce. Consider local Realtor associations, neighborhood associations, public interest clubs and more.

Each of these groups has an active, passionate group of individuals who want to know more about things you offer, and you sell.

What's more, most of these clubs and associations will have Web sites that are hubs of activity for members in between meetings. This is a big opportunity for you to get your Web site linked in front of club & association members, driving more members to discover and visit your business online.

Other ways to get involved and drive customer activity from these groups:

Attend Meetings: Introduce yourself, tell people what you do, and invite them to come visit you online. Hand out business cards with your Web address prominently mentioned.

Offer to Present Something: Club and association leaders are always looking for good content to present at meetings. What do you know that could be of interest to members? Getting 15-20 minutes in front of this valuable audience can be easier than you think!

Offer to Host a Meeting: Why not host a meeting at your office or retail location? It's an easy way to make sure you get time on the agenda to present as well, plus a great way for people to learn more directly about your business.

Create a Special Page for the Group on your Web Site: If the association doesn't yet have a Web site, why not offer to host information for the group on a page on your Web site?

Promote the association in your newsletter, blog or podcast: The more you do this, the more the club or association will also promote your business to its members.

The possibilities are endless. And if your interest in the club or associations is genuine, this is a great way to meet a large group of new customers, participate in their cause, and drive both them and their networks to your business.

STEP FORTY ACTION ITEMS:
Find local, related clubs & associations.
Find ways to participate!

Step 41: Start a social group or network

Discovering and leveraging existing clubs, associations and networks is a big opportunity. But why not start your own? Why not facilitate a group of people that care about what you're selling, in a group hosted by you?

What better way to get a network of interested, current and prospective customers to interact with your company – both online and in person? These social groups can take all shapes. If you operate a bakery, why not start a local cooking club?

Does your community have a neighborhood association? If not, and you're a real estate agent, why not start one? Could you create and facilitate a social group among residents of your neighborhood?

If you own a pet store, why not organize get-togethers of pets (and their owners)? Could you facilitate the online sharing of stories, nutritional tips, and other information?

All of these groups can mean both online and offline gatherings. Clearly it will make sense to gather your new social group together occasionally in person. But many more group "meetings" will happen online. Group members can get together anytime in an online discussion group, post things for and with each other on a blog, and more.

And all of these online activities can be hosted by you – on your Web site and your blog.

The possibilities are endless. Think through the kind of social groups and networks that might make sense for your business. If those groups are already in existence, then by all means – participate.

But if they're not yet available to members of your community, get them started!

STEP FORTY ONE ACTION ITEMS:
Start a social group for your business!
Host online gathering and information sharing among members on your Web site.

Step 42: Blogger communities

Do a quick search on Google Blogsearch or Technorati for keywords associated with your business or industry, and you're bound to find several already-active blogs, written by local consumers. Many of these blogs are already visited by other potential customers in and around your community.

At the same time that you create and foster your own blog, make sure you're building relationships with other bloggers in your community and industry.

If you find other local bloggers writing about real estate, call them up and introduce yourself. Talk to them about what they write about, what they're interested in, and offer content and advice from your own business.
This will encourage the existing bloggers to write about (and link to) your business with their readers.

Step 43: Blog comments galore!

If you've started a blog as part of your online publishing strategy, these next two steps represent the best way to quickly start driving traffic back to your new blog.

The first step is to participate in other blogs. Find conversations going on elsewhere that you have an opinion on, and make a comment.

This can be on blogs directly related to your industry or business, or it can simply be on blogs that happen to mention things you care about.

Most blogs ask for (and some require) a Web site when posting a comment, which is a great way to drive traffic back to your own Web site or blog.

Better yet, embed a link to a specific article or piece of content on your own Web site or blog that furthers the point you're making in the other blog's comments section.

This works particularly well when you're paying close attention to some of the most well-read blogs in your area.

Take the Kirkland Weblog mentioned earlier in the book, for example. It's one of the most well-read blogs in the Kirkland area, primarily read by Kirkland residents and other small businesses.

In addition to building a relationship with the bloggers themselves, stay active in their comments section. Bloggers love to have others comment on what they've written about, and it's a great way to 1) drive traffic back to your own site, and 2) further a relationship you may have with that blogger, which will only mean more mentions and links down the road.

STEP FORTY THREE ACTION ITEMS:
Find active blog posts writing about things you're interested in.
Comment back, and include links to your Web site or blog.

Step 44: Your blogroll (and the blogrolls of others)

A blogroll, quite simply, is a list of blogs.

For many bloggers, their blogroll represents a list of other bloggers they admire, and blogs they read on a frequent basis. Blogrolls tend to represent a short list of sites that the particular blogger "recommends" to his or her readers.

There are two ways to take advantage of blogrolls:

1. Start your own, and let people know about it
2. Get yourself on other bloggers' blogrolls

As you notice blogs that you like – either bloggers in your community, or others in your industry, or fellow businesses – put together your own blogroll.

Post your blogroll on your Web site, or on the sidebar of your blog (Blogger and WordPress software makes these very easy to build).

Then, when you're finished, email the bloggers you've included and tell them they're now in your blogroll.

The bloggers will greatly appreciate being included, and very well may include you as well in their own blogrolls.

But the biggest key to getting onto blogrolls is to write great blogs, and share those blog posts with others.

Let's say you're a real estate agent, and have written a short blog post about how consumers are using the Internet to search for homes. What if you shared that blog post with other real estate technology companies, especially any companies that you mentioned in your post? What if you shared it with other real estate bloggers that you know care particularly deeply about technology?

The best way to get noticed by other bloggers is to either write about things they care about, or to mention them directly in your blog posts. And when you do one or both of these things, you're likelihood of being included in their blog-roll goes up significantly.

STEP FORTY FOUR ACTION ITEMS:
Start a blogroll.
Tell others about it.

Step 45: Write a column (you can do it!)

If you're already a blogger, then you're a short step away from being a columnist. You're also not far away from being a full-fledged book author, but we'll get to that at the end of this book.

The typical blog post is between 50-150 words. The typical Letter to the Editor is 250-300 words.

The typical newspaper or magazine column is 600-1,000 words. Flesh out your ideas a bit more (add a couple examples or additional insights/ anecdotes) and you've taken a good blog post or Letter to the Editor into column territory.

You'd also be surprised how easy it can be to get your column published. Local newspaper editors are typically hungry for content, especially if they can get well-written content for free.

But the local newspaper isn't the only place you can get a column published. Other potential publishing vehicles include:

    The Chamber of Commerce newsletter
    The local PTA newsletter
    The neighborhood association's Web site or newsletter
    The city's newsletter or Web site
    Local club or association publications

Know your audience, and know where they get their information. Then find the editor of that source, and offer your content. If you have well-articulated, well-written content, chances are you'll get published.

Step 46: Join referral networks

Would you pay for a referral? Of course you would.

Unfortunately, most businesses don't have a formal referral compensation plan, and don't have a regular referral network in which to share customers with other businesses.

There are several places online that businesses in all industries can leverage to send and receive referrals. In fact, some of the businesses you already work with may already offer a referral network, some you didn't know about and haven't yet used.

Take the Chamber of Commerce, for example. Your local Chamber would be happy to help facilitate referrals for you with other related businesses.

Are you in real estate? Did you know that HouseValues offers a robust referral network for all of its nationwide customers, enabling agents across town and across the country to share referrals with each other?

If you're a contractor or in the home improvement space, there are several online referral networks you can join. For a fee (either flat referral fee or a commission), you can often sign up for and receive numerous referrals each month.

There's clearly an opportunity here to create your own referral network as well. If you do this, make sure you're thinking through how referring companies would want to be compensated, and make it worth their while (while protecting your own interests and profitability).

But at a minimum, research and take advantage of existing referral networks, most of which already exist online and are ripe for the taking.

Step 47: Letters to the Editor

Despite the growth and sophistication of conversations online, Letters to the Editor (to newspapers and magazines) are still a powerful opportunity for individuals and companies to express their ideas, establish credibility and thought leadership, and drive direct interest and traffic back to their businesses.

For local businesses, the opportunity to leverage Letters to the Editor is even more real, and easier to achieve.

Most small-market and neighborhood newspapers don't get nearly the same volume of letters as the bigger city newspapers, and therefore are more apt to accept and publish well-written letters that articulately discuss a subject of interest to local readers.

Even better, most newspapers accept letters via email, so writing a Letter to the Editor is now as easy as writing an email.

Just choose your subject wisely. It's probably not a good idea to treat a Letter to the Editor like a press release. Editors aren't going to publish a letter you write advertising new products, or an upcoming open house.

Rather, choose a subject that's already "in the news" and in the hearts & minds of your local audience. Then write your opinion on the matter.

Most newspapers limit Letters to the Editor to just 200-300 words, so be succinct.

When your letter is published, you'll be surprised how many phone calls and Web site visits you receive as a result.

STEP FORTY SEVEN ACTION ITEMS:
Pick a subject your local audience is particularly interested in.
Write a Letter to the Editor (start with your neighborhood newspaper).

Step 48: Are you available?

When customers call, do you answer the phone? When they come visit your store, do you greet them immediately?

When they leave you a voicemail, do you return it within an hour or two? When your customers send you an email, are you quick with a response?

That's what "being available" is all about. If you're a small business, and your customers know that, then responses in the middle of the night probably aren't expected.

But if it's the middle of the business day, and a customer sends an inquiry (via phone, email, via your Web site, etc.), they expect a fast response.

In the electronically-enabled world that we live in, your customers expect immediate responses to their questions.

By following up as quickly as possible, you're increasing not only the likelihood that those customers are going to stay customers, but also the possibility that they'll refer you to friends and family as well.

Now, how can your Web site enable more immediate availability with your customers? Here are a couple ways:

> **Instant Chat:** There are companies online that will allow you to place a "chat" service right on your Web site or blog, so that customers can see when you're online and chat with you immediately.

> **Instant Messenger:** Put your best customers in your Instant Messenger network, so that they can also chat with you in real-time when you're online.

> **Click-to-Call:** Several companies, including RingCentral, enable software that will directly connect you with your customers, just by having your customers click a button on your Web site. When the customer clicks a button and enters their phone number online, the service directly calls your phone and connects you with the customer. Instant phone calls, initiated online.

These are three great ways to immediately connect live with your customers online.

Another way to service your customers immediately online is with several "self-help" tools.

For example, ever notice that customers often call or email with the same questions over and over? Why not answer those questions online. Create a "Frequently Asked Questions" list right on your Web site, so that customers can easily find and get answers for their "most-asked" questions.

STEP FORTY EIGHT ACTION ITEMS:
Be available to your customers (within reason).
Use new online tools to directly connect customers to you.
Anticipate their questions, and answer them online.

Step 49: What's your response time?

Numerous polls of Internet-savvy consumers tell us that they want instant responses to their questions.

However, they don't always get what they want, and this has created a gap between desires and expectations.

Put another way, consumers *demand* instant response times to their questions (especially when delivered online or via email), but they rarely *expect* such great service.

Now imagine the impression you'll give those customers when you respond quickly.

When someone visits your Web site and makes a request (either via email or an online request form), what do you think will happen when you get back to them within the hour?

What do you think would happen if you called them within 10-15 minutes to clarify their request and give an answer?

Your customer will be amazed. They'll tell their friends. You'll be offering incredible customer service, initiated and facilitated by your Web site.

It'll create new customers, delight your current customers, and drive even more transactions and interactions with your business through your Web site.

Just by responding to questions quickly. Imagine that.

STEP FORTY NINE ACTION ITEMS:
Respond quickly.

Step 50: Radio show call-ins

In Seattle, best-selling real estate author and former *Seattle Times* real estate editor Tom Kelly hosts a weekly radio show called Real Estate Today. It's recorded live each Sunday morning from a studio in downtown Seattle, broadcast on one of the popular local AM stations, and then rebroadcast on business radio stations across the country.

Each week, Tom features some great information for consumers about real estate-related topics. Each week, he invites callers to call and ask questions, and also to share their own real estate-related stories.

Tom does a great job with this program, and has a huge following both in Seattle and across the country.

And it shocks me that, despite his show's popularity and enormous opportunity, I never hear real estate agents calling in to ask questions or share their insights.

Radio show call-ins are the next best thing to actually being featured on the radio show itself. And it's the audio version of the Letter to the Editor we discussed earlier.

Almost every market has a real estate radio show on weekends. If you're in real estate, you should listen and participate regularly.

But any business owner can call in on virtually any topic with talk radio, as long as it's relevant to listeners. Don't be afraid to give a plug for more information on your Web site, too.

STEP FIFTY ACTION ITEMS:
Find relevant content on the radio.
Call in and participate!

Step 51: Supporting other local businesses

You do for me, I'll do for you.

For many individuals and businesses, this comes naturally. For others, it takes focus.

Either way, go out of your way as often as possible to help those around you.

This can take many shapes, including:

Promoting other businesses on your Web site or blog
Putting their coupons and special offers in your own shopping bags
Sharing customers via a referral program
Organizing or participating in local business best practice sharing sessions

Because what goes around, comes around. The more you share with others, the more they'll share with you.

STEP FIFTY ONE ACTION ITEMS:
Do the right thing for other local businesses.

Step 52: Host a seminar

Here's a great opportunity to start a conversation offline, and continue it indefinitely online.

Think through not only what your customers buy from you, but what they're broadly interested in. What can you teach them that they don't already know? What can you share that will help heighten their enjoyment of what you sell, or get them even more interested in your industry or category?

If you're thinking of hosting a seminar, remember that the speaker doesn't have to be you.

For example, if you're a real estate agent specializing in first-time home buyers, you have a vested interested in helping renters understand that they can probably afford far more house than they think.

So, why not hire a financial planner for a day to conduct a seminar teaching renters how to manage their finances, and built up enough savings for a down payment on a house?

Most content from a seminar can also be repurposed online. For example, every live event can be translated into:

A document summarizing the main points of the seminar

A podcast of the audio feed

An online video of the entire seminar

A blog post & discussion on related topics (including testimonials from those who attended the live seminar)

By hosting a great seminar, you'll have tons of content you can repurpose and leverage online for weeks and months to come.

STEP FIFTY TWO ACTION ITEMS:
Consider hosting a seminar.
Find the right speaker (it might not be you!)

Step 53: Host a how-to workshop

I believe that a "how-to" workshop is very different from a seminar.

When I think seminar, I think about someone speaking to me, lecturing, teaching me something interesting in a largely one-way format.

When I think "how-to" workshop, I think about something far more interactive, hands-on, and with more two-way interaction between speaker/presenter and participants.

If you run a small business, and have loyal customers already, then clearly you have a skill that others need. In most cases, your customers would probably love to hear you teach them a little of your own knowledge.

And chances are, you aren't even thinking about the knowledge you have, and how others could be drawn to it (both current and prospective customers).

The opportunities here are endless. Some "how-to" workshop possibilities include:

Cooking classes for bakers, restaurant owners and caterers

Home improvement workshops conducted by general contractors, or even plumbers, roofers and other home services providers

Woodworking classes by the local hardware store

For every one of these workshop opportunities, there are countless ways to leverage the content to drive traffic and business directly to your Web site. These include:

Downloadable course outlines or workbooks

Ongoing instruction or Q&A availablity online from the instructors afterward

Sharing of customer projects completed after the class (in video or photo format)

An ongoing series of podcasts related to the initial workshop

STEP FIFTY THREE ACTION ITEMS:
Try hosting a "how-to" workshop.
Think about ways to leverage the content and subject matter online.

Step 54: Survey, survey, survey

Surveys can be great research tools to gain greater insight into your customers, but can also be leveraged to drive greater interest and traffic back to your business and Web site.

For example, let's say you're a real estate agent. You want to know how your customers are feeling about today's real estate market, what they think about interest rates, and whether or not they're thinking about investing in real estate.

So you put together a survey. You can build online surveys for free on various survey Web sites. I recommend SurveyMonkey.com and Zoomerang.com for quick, easy-to-build surveys that can be sent via email, or linked right on your Web site or blog.

Write your questions carefully, then poll your customers. It's a great way to get them engaged on your Web site, and learn more about how you can better deliver service back to your customers.

Better yet, your customers will appreciate that you care about them, and care enough to ask their opinion in the first place.

What you get back should help you craft better messaging, products and services for your customers.

But that's not the end of this story.

The insight you have is quite valuable, and some might be worth sharing with others.

Consider announcing some of your survey results on your Web site or blog. Or perhaps the results are worth putting into a press release or newspaper column.

Tease results from the survey through these channels, and invite readers & listeners to come to your Web site to read more.

You'll demonstrate considerable thought leadership for having conducted the survey and shared the insights in the first place, and you'll be giving your business significant added visibility and traffic.

Step 55: Charities

People like supporting charities, and also feel good about supporting businesses that support charities.

If you have a genuine interest in supporting others, and helping your customers do the same, you can use this to your advantage.

As with most ideas in this book, there are countless ways this can take shape. Some possibilities include:

During a certain promotional period, you'll donate a percentage from all sales to a particular needy charity

Partner with a local charity to help them out (with money, time or talents) in exchange for their promotion of your business and Web site in their own marketing materials and mailers

Tell Web site visitors that you'll donate a dollar to a favorite charity for every customer who signs up for your new email newsletter

Volunteer yourself and your employees to spend time helping a local charity, and encourage your customers to do the same (better yet, do it together! An example of this could be a Habitat for Humanity home-building projects that you and your customers do together)

Find the charity that fits you best, and the opportunity in your business that you feel most comfortable with. I can't stress enough how important authenticity is in working with charities in your marketing plan.

If you are truly genuine about your interest, and that shows to your customers, this can be an incredibly powerful driver of new customers, as well as current customer loyalty.

FIVE: PRODUCTIVITY

You're running a successful business. Keeping everything going. Doing a million things at once.

How do you keep yourself organized? Most business owners I know have their own methods and systems of staying organized, but few believe they have things nailed.

And now that we've started patterns of online marketing that will exponentially grow your business, keeping yourself organized just got a lot harder.

Not only do you have a bunch of new marketing ideas to execute and keep going, but you're going to have a LOT more business to take care of as well.

Being organized and productive will be more important than ever before from this day forward.

What follows are several proven strategies I've found for myself, or learned from others, that can help keep you organized, and focused on doing the right things for your business.

Step 56: Task List

As part of my New Year's Resolutions this past year, I'm trying to get better organized - both in my professional and personal life. Like you, I find I'm constantly pulled in a thousand different directions, and have a hard time

1) remembering everything I need to do (or want to do), and 2) putting them in a good, priority order so that the most important things are getting done first.

One of the things I've started doing is making extensive use of the "tasks" feature in Microsoft Outlook. I've used this feature on and off for years, but just recently have started making it a regular part of my organizational structure.

In the past, I've kept primarily work-related items in my Task list. Now, I'm starting to keep track of everything.

Yes, my work priorities and deliverables are all there, divided by functional responsibility. But I'm also tracking my "honey do" list for projects around the house. I'm tracking my progressive shopping list for weekend trips to The Home Depot. Calls I need to return (personal and professional). Books I want to read (and either purchase or check-out from the local library). Personal errands. Even an inventory of future blog posts, columns to write, and new book ideas.

It's all organized as Tasks.

This may seem like overkill, but I now have (on one piece of paper) an inventory of things across my life that are important to me, and that I want to get done.

The best way to remember to get something done is to write it down. And I've found that, by writing things down in a single, organized place, I can quickly reference the list and be far more efficient with my time getting things done.

STEP FIFTY SIX ACTION ITEMS:
Start a task list.
Include everything.

Step 57: Top Five and "One of Five"

Making lists of the things I need to do, and aggregating those lists in one place, has been quite helpful in increasing my productivity.

Getting more things done is a good first step. But I'm also getting more of the right things done, thanks to a daily "top five" list.

Let's first assume that you've set explicit goals for this year, and this quarter.

If you know what success looks like at the end of this quarter and year, you should be able to map that back into weekly, even daily, deliverables for yourself and your team.

And that's where the top five, and "first of five", come in.

Many people set priorities, but fail to effectively prioritize the priorities. If I have five priorities today, and get two of them done, were those the most important two priorities to get done? Did you get done the most important priority today?

With the myriad things on our plates each day, it's easy to focus on some of the easiest projects, or the emails in front of us, or simply be reactive to what appears the most urgent. But if we look back, that work rarely maps to the most important, most direct means of achieving our monthly, quarterly and annual objectives.

So now, every morning, I establish my top five priorities for the day. And I focus on achieving the priority at the top of the list. If I've prioritized correctly, I'm spending my time on the most important project - that day, and every day.

Tomorrow, the list simply shifts up. Today's #2 priority (assuming it didn't get done) becomes tomorrow's "first of five", and gets done.

Lists are important. Prioritized lists are better. And getting the most important priority done each day is far better than simply getting "a lot done."

STEP FIFTY SEVEN ACTION ITEMS:
Prioritize your list into your "top five".
Pick your "one of five" each day, and get it done – every day.

Step 58: Blackberries (not the fruit)

Every business owner should have access to email remotely. Even if you work in retail and are close to your computer and email relatively often, you can greatly improve your inquiry response time with a mobile email device.

Greater communication mobility can not only help you communicate easier and faster with customers and suppliers, but also enables other technology that speeds up your communication even further.

For example, HouseValues operates a customer management software system for its real estate professional customers, and notifies customers when they get a new customer inquiry into the system.

HouseValues sends its customers what they call a "Money Call", meaning a customer has just submitted a request and is awaiting a response.

If you're an agent and out in the field, you can respond to that customer right away with such technology (vs. waiting until you're back at the office and on your computer again).

STEP FIFTY EIGHT ACTION ITEMS:
Get a mobile email device.
Use it often to stay in touch with customers.

Step 59: Jott.com

You're in the car, at the mall, or just plain away from your computer. But you have an idea, remember a to-do, and have your cell phone handy.

In the past, you might have left yourself a voicemail, then gone in and written down those voicemail to-do's.

Now, a new service called Jott eliminates the middle step, by sending those voicemails in text format straight to your email inbox. You can also organize your to-do list right in Jott.com, and "Jottcast" your to-do's to others in your Jott network.

For those who regularly think about, and then forget, things on the road or away from a computer or note pad, this is a great new (and free) service.

Worth checking out at Jott.com.

Step 60: Grand Central

You're a small business, and use several different phone numbers throughout the day. You have a home phone, a work phone, and a cell phone. You can never remember which one was given to different customers, suppliers and partners.

You want one number that reaches you everywhere – your cell phone, your work phone, or your home phone.

When customers call, you want to make sure you get that call.

That's what GrandCentral.com is for. It's a new service with some fantastic features, all focused on helping ensure that you never miss another call again.

It's a great way to save money (i.e. pick up the work phone instead of your cell phone to save minutes), and also a great way to ensure you don't miss an important call again.

Step 61: SiteMeter.com

Free Web site and blog tracking. That's what SiteMeter.com offers.

Sign up is fast, easy and free. Simply add a small set of code to your Web site or blog (SiteMeter shows you how), and you're in business.

Then, log onto SiteMeter's Web site to see stats such as:

> How much traffic you've received the past hour, today, this week and this month

Where that traffic is coming from
What articles they're viewing
Which search engines and search terms they're using

You can sign up for the "deluxe" package of statistics for just $7/month, but I've found the free stats are plenty for most small business Web sites and blogs. Worth a look.

STEP SIXTY ONE ACTION ITEMS:
Sign up for a free SiteMeter.com account.

SIX: LEARNING

I hope that the ideas and insights in this book will inspire you to start and keep up with an aggressive, profitable Web marketing strategy.

But as soon as I'm done typing the final chapter, something new will have popped up.

A new idea, a new technology, or a new service that should have been included here, and should be something you explore and try using to improve your Web marketing strategy.

That's what this section is all about. Part of your job as a marketer and business manager is to
continue learning, and continue gaining insights that will keep the customers coming back again and again.

Eventually, we may write the next edition of this book with some of those new ideas. In the meantime, here are several ways to find them first.

Step 62: Other blogs

Ten years ago, to get great marketing ideas and insights from the industry's most creative thinkers, you had to buy a magazine subscription. Not anymore.

Many of the best new ideas, best creative thinking, and breakthrough new ideas are being shared every day, for free, on blogs.

They're out there every day for the taking. Whether you commit to reading certain blogs every day, or just visit a few once in awhile, you'll be a richer marketer and smarter business owner as a result.

But which blogs are worth reading? Of the millions being published every day, how do you know which will be most worth your time?

That's a question only you can answer. But as far as helping you grow your business, and expend the value of your Web marketing strategy, I recommend looking in two categories.

Marketing Blogs
There are some great marketing bloggers out there – Seth Godin, Jackie Huba, John Jantsch and more. I've included many of my favorite marketing bloggers on my own blogroll, available here:

http://www.bloglines.com/public/mattonmarketing

I invite you to browse what's available there, and choose a few that specifically connect with the way you already think.

Plus, many of these blogs will link you to other blogs worth discovering. Every day, new marketing "voices" join the conversation and offer new insights we hadn't yet thought of. Those new voices are worth listening to.

Industry Blogs
Who else is blogging in your industry? And what can you learn from them?

My blogroll above includes several blogs in the real estate industry, many of which should be required reading for real estate agents looking to keep an edge for their Web marketing strategy.

But no matter what your industry, find out who else is blogging – fellow business owners, consultants and service providers that cater to your industry. Put those folks in your own blogroll, and over time introduce yourself.

The best way to keep track of all your blogs is to use Bloglines.com. It's a free service that will aggregate "feeds" from each of your blogs. What does that mean? Instead of visiting dozens of different sites to see what's new, you visit just ONE site, and it tells you which of your favorite blogs have been recently updated. It's a great time saver.

STEP SIXTY TWO ACTION ITEMS:
Start reading marketing and industry blogs.
Sign up for a Bloglines.com account to keep track of your favorite blogs.

Step 63: Read the right books!

Listed below are several books that I recommend both to improve your Web marketing skills and to help you think like a marketing leader.

Of course, this is but a small sample of the wide variety of great business books out there to read.

I read far fewer business books these days than five years ago, largely because there's so much great content available for free online – via email newsletters, blogs and more.

But what I do recommend is that you make good use of your local public library. I check business and marketing books out from the library quite often, mostly to "test them out" and see if I want to spend more time with them.

If I really like the book, I might go out and buy myself a copy. Otherwise, I give it a quick skim for good ideas, or read it quickly and return it. It's the best way to get access to all of the great business books published each year, and not pay a dime!

That said, if you're ready to start a marketing library, here are my recommendations. These are the books in my bookshelf with the most highlights, notes and dog-ears – meaning I not only have read them multiple times, but still refer to them regularly for good ideas and refreshers.

All Marketers Are Liars
By Seth Godin

Creating Customer Evangelists
By Ben Mc Connell and Jackie Huba

Word-of-Mouth Marketing
By Andy Sernovitz

The Anatomy of Buzz
By Emanuel Rosen

Mastering the Rockefeller Habits
By Verne Harnish

What Clients Love: A Field Guide to Growing Your Business
By Harry Beckwith

Zingerman's Guide to Giving Great Service
By Ari Weinzweig

STEP SIXTY THREE ACTION ITEMS:
Pick some good books to read.
Use your local library to explore more, for free!

Step 64: Email newsletters

Sure, we all get far too much email. But the most successful business owners know that within that flood of emails are extremely valuable nuggets of information – marketing ideas, best practices, new product opportunities and much more.

Let's talk first about spam. I'm talking about all of the unsolicited emails we get every day.

Much of this spam is truly worthless. But be careful not to quickly delete the business-related stuff you get – things you may receive because you somehow got added to a business email list a few months ago.

Some of the most successful business owners know that there's diamonds in the rough here. They know that for every 19 worthless spam emails, there's typically one that will teach them something, that will introduce a new concept, or that will spark an idea that can truly impact their business.

There are also a number of great email newsletters out there worth investigating. Be sure to look for those that are specific to your industry, but here are a few I also recommend that are more generally about marketing.

I've included an easy URL next to each newsletter name, so you can quickly visit and sign up.

They vary in frequency – from daily to monthly – and you don't need to read every issue. I personally subscribe to more than 40 email newsletters, of varying frequencies, and don't come close to reading every issue.

But what I do read enriches my professional work. Even if you only commit a few minutes a day to scan these newsletters, you'll find the investment is worth your time.

> The Monday Morning Memo
> http://www.mondaymorningmemo.com
>
> MarketingProfs Today
> http://www.marketingprofs.com
>
> MarketingSherpa
> http://www.marketingsherpa.com
>
> Verne Harnish's Weekly Insights
> http://www.gazelles.com
>
> ClickZ Experts
> http://www.clickz.com

STEP SIXTY FOUR ACTION ITEMS:
Sign up for several email newsletters.
Read them when you have time.
Scan your spam for diamonds!

Step 65: Your social networks

We've discussed already how to promote your business and your Web site through various professional networks – clubs, associations, the local Chamber of Commerce, etc.

But at the same time that you're using these channels to market your business, make sure you're learning from other members as well.

Chances are, once you've completed just a portion of the steps in this book, you'll be light years ahead of your colleagues in terms of creating and building a profitable Web marketing strategy. But there's still plenty to learn from your colleagues.

For example, many recommendations in this book simply take existing, offline marketing and sales channels, and extend their leverage to drive traffic to your Web site.

Pay close attention to what others in your professional networks are doing to promote their business, and think about 1) what those things could do for your business, and 2) how you would leverage them to promote your Web site, email newsletter, blog or podcast.

Investing more time with your professional networks will also make it far easier to ask colleagues and peers for their help in marketing your business. If they see you more often, and you're actively participating in your shared network, they're far more likely to help you than if they never see you, and you only stop by when you want something.

STEP SIXTY FIVE ACTION ITEMS:
Participate in your professional networks more regularly.
Learn from what your peers are doing, both online and offline.

Step 66: Podcasts

Podcasts were built for multi-tasking.

Just like books on tape. Most people don't settle onto the couch at home, pop in a book on tape, and listen for a couple hours. People buy books on tape for the car, for travel, or for the gym. It's a great way to catch up on a book when you don't otherwise had time to read the "traditional" way.

Podcasts are no different. I've found podcasts to be perfect for the gym, for example. I'm focused on the words and conversation, which makes my time on the Stairclimber go that much faster.

If you're still relatively new to podcasts, I'd encourage you to browse the selection on iTunes, or use one of the fantastic new podcast search engines (such as Pluggd) to find content fit for your interests. Here are five of my favorites (you can find them all on iTunes and Pluggd.com):

The New York Times Front Page: In five minutes or less, a nice man reads me the stories from the paper's front page, plus offers a little perspective on each story beyond the headlines. A great way to get caught up quickly on national and world news, and it fits into even the shortest morning commutes! It's one of several podcasts offered by the Times.

Duct-Tape Marketing Podcast: I'm a big fan of what John Jantsch is doing on his Web site and blog, and he's now extended it to a series of podcasts. Most feature interviews with some of marketing's top minds, all focused on providing listeners with real-life, tangible marketing ideas that can immediately be put to work in almost any business.

HBR Ideacast: The editors of Harvard Business Review bring their journal to life in this great podcast, featuring a mix of outside speakers, HBS professors and other luminaries sharing a combination of business strategy, marketing insights, and collected best practices. Just like the magazine, this podcast will help you keep a strategic edge.

Marketing Voices: One of several great podcasts from PodTech.net, this one features Jennifer Jones interviewing a wide variety of marketing and technology leaders on subjects relevant to all of us.

The Wood Whisperer: This is unrelated to marketing, and a video podcast to-boot, but it's just plain cool. I'm a budding (but very amateur) wordworker these days, and Marc does a great job explaining everything from how to use tools to how to build boxes. It's a great example of how video podcasting can work, and also an example of just how much great content is out there already.

STEP SIXTY SIX ACTION ITEMS:
Try out some podcasts.
Search for some relevant to your industry on Pluggd.com.

Step 67: Mystery shopping

The best, most direct, most efficient way to see exactly how your peers, competitors and colleagues treat their customers is to become a customer yourself.

What does that mean? Do any or all of the following:

    Visit their Web site
    Buy something from them online
    Email them to see how (and when, and how quickly) they respond
    Sign up for their mailing list

Now that you've become a Web marketing expert, you'll likely be underwhelmed by what you see from others.

But you'll also gain a unique perspective on not only things you can improve on in your own business, but also which parts of your customer strategy are most important, and might need the most work.

Make "mystery shopping" a regular thing. Commit to shopping at 1-2 new businesses each week.

They don't all need to be competitors. They can be peers, friends, or just businesses you're interested in.

But learning direct from other businesses is often a great way to accelerate growth and performance in your own business.

STEP SIXTY SEVEN ACTION ITEMS:
Become a customer of your competitors.
Learn from what they do well (and especially from what they don't do well).

Step 68: Other successful businesses like you!

In addition to mystery shopping, you should pay particularly close attention to the businesses like yours that are doing well.

This might mean another bakery around town, or a top-producing real estate agent in your neighborhood.

But it might also mean a business across the country, one that you found online and have admired from afar.

Dig into what they're doing, introduce yourself to the business owners, and figure out what makes them so successful.

Imitation is indeed a sincere form of flattery, and there's nothing stopping you from emulating the best practices of other businesses in your field.

In fact, it's through emulation and improvement that most companies catapult themselves into greater levels of success and profitability.

> **STEP SIXTY EIGHT ACTION ITEMS:**
> Find other businesses like yours that are seeing success.
> Meet them, and emulate them.

Step 69: Surprise Networking

Want to meet new people? Expand your network? Part of the solution is right in front of you.

Let's say you read an article in the paper, online or in a magazine about an interesting company. An executive from the company is interviewed for the story. Why not write an email to the executive, introducing yourself and expressing your interest and delight in the story you just read?

You'll get more responses than you think.

Let's say you hear an interview on the radio, or on a podcast. Why not write an email to the interviewee, thanking them for their insights?

Sending a quick "thank you" or "appreciated your ideas" note is faster and easier than ever, thanks to email. And thanks to the Internet, finding contact information for those executives and interviewees is also quite easy.

So here's my challenge to you this week. Send an email to five people you don't know. Just five. Do it based on things you read, things you hear, or just businesses you've always admired.

The Internet is a virtual cocktail reception. If you summon the courage to walk up to someone and introduce yourself, well, you've just made a new friend, and expanded your network.

STEP SIXTY NINE ACTION ITEMS:
Introduce yourself to people you don't know.
Do it often!

SEVEN: PURE GUERILLA

This last section is where we stuffed the ideas that didn't naturally fit in the previous sections, but that we just couldn't leave out of the book.

They're great, guerilla marketing tactics that every business should be using.

This section, of course, is far too short. It's just a small, small sample of the millions of guerilla marketing tactics being used across the country, by small businesses every day, to generate more business for themselves – online and offline.

Start with these six ideas, then innovate more on your own.

Step 70: Hand-written notes

Most of what we receive these days – at work and at home – is type-written. We get plenty of electronic messages and emails, and most of our postage-mail is even type-written.

When we receive a hand-written note, it stands out.

Make your business stand out with the occasional hand-written note. It can be a thank you, a congratulations, or just a "thinking about you" to a special customer.

Try sending just 1-2 notes a day. Include a coupon, or business card, or even a hand-written invitation to visit your Web site.

I guarantee you'll be amazed by the response. Not enough people write notes by hand anymore. Take advantage of that scarcity to make your business stand out.

STEP SEVENTY ACTION ITEMS:
Write 1-2 hand-written notes per day.

Step 71: Mail a news clipping

Read your local newspaper voraciously. Look for mentions of your colleagues, peers, professional network associates, and customers.

You're more likely to find mentions of your professional peers – instances where they're quoted in an article, or featured in a news release, etc. Or you might find an advertisement they've placed that you think is particularly well done.

Less likely but arguably more important are mentions of your customers.

It could be that a customer's son is written up for a Little League game. Or that a daughter was a star performer in the local school play.

When you find stories (or ads) from people and businesses you know, clip them out and send them with a quick hand-written note of congratulations.

This will show your customers and colleagues that you noticed, and you care.

It's another step you can take to make your business remarkable, stand out from others, and drive more word-of-mouth that will bring more bodies through the door.

STEP SEVENTY ONE ACTION ITEMS:
Search the local newspaper for mentions of customers and colleagues.
Clip them and mail them.

Step 72: Create a trivia contest

Many businesses already use this as an awareness and traffic-building tactic, primarily because trivia contests never seem to get old.

A coffee stand next to my home offers a daily trivia question. I've talked to many coffee drinkers who typically use the nearby Starbucks, but occasionally visit this specific coffee stand because they know the answer to the trivia question. The fact that they get 50 cents off their latte is secondary; what's most important is that the question itself got their attention, and made them stop for a purchase.

Many pubs and restaurants use this tactic as well, sponsoring a regular "trivia night" for teams to come in and compete against each other. It's a great way to get patrons to stay for awhile, order more drinks and food, etc.

How could trivia work in your business? Many, many ways. Here are a few examples:

> Post a trivia question on your Web site, and tell visitors that they'll get a discount (or a freebie!) when they come into the store with the answer
>
> Focus trivia questions on your product line, something that requires customers to learn more about products you sell to find the answer, and redeem the answer for a prize (a discount, a freebie, etc.)
>
> Create a progressive trivia contest, with a new question posted each week. After a period of time, the customers with the most correct answers get a prize. This will keep customers engaged with your business, plus encourage repeat visitations and purchases

Every business is unique, including the application of trivia contests to drive intrigue, engagement and retention of customers – both online and offline.

STEP SEVENTY TWO ACTION ITEMS:
Try a trivia contest with your customers.
Give them something for coming up with the right answer.

Step 73: Gift certificates

Remember your freebies?

If you're a real estate agent, you'd gladly give new prospective customers a free CMA. If you're a baker, maybe you'll give a new customer a free cookie.

Or it can be one of the many "special reports" and other freebies you've created – things that didn't cost you much, but have high value among customers and prospects.

Why not create gift certificates for customers to use & redeem for those freebies?

The gift certificate itself will imply higher value in the giveaway, and will help drive more customers to redeem the certificate.

Better yet, give your customers multiple gift certificates so they can pass them along to their friends and family.

STEP SEVENTY THREE ACTION ITEMS:
Create gift certificates for your freebies.

Step 74: Meet your neighbors!

I'm not talking about your business neighbors, I mean the people you live next to. Do you know them? Do they know you? Do they know what you do for a living?

Every neighbor is a potential customer. That doesn't mean you're going door-to-door pitching your wares, or treating the neighborhood BBQ like a Pampered Chef event.

But it does mean your neighbors should hear about your business when you have a chance. Every neighbor also has a network. They know people at church, at their kids' school, on the Little League sidelines. Activate that network.

STEP SEVENTY FOUR ACTION ITEMS:
Know your neighbors (at home, not just at work).
Make sure they know what you do for a living!

Step 75: Write a book

Want to be perceived quickly as an expert in your field? Write the book about it.

Want to convince a client that you're the best choice for their next job? Show them your book.

Are you a real estate agent who wants to differentiate yourself from the competition? Write a book about home buying and selling, or about neighborhoods in your area.

Pick a topic you're passionate about, related to your business, and write about it.

Now, writing a book is obviously far more complicated than writing a press release, or newspaper column. Those marketing tools can be completed in a day.

Writing a book will take you weeks, possibly months.

But if you take it step-by-step, it can be done.

Want help? Get inspiration from Ann McIndoo, and her great Web site at http://www.SoYouWantToWrite.com. She breaks the book-writing process down into smaller, accessible steps that work. She also offers some great resources to help you along the way.

One she introduced me to is LuLu.com, a self-publishing tool that will help you print your new book on-demand, in whatever quantity you want.

Want just 50 copies? LuLu.com can do it. Cheaper than you think.

Getting your book posted on Amazon.com is also easy. Just set up an Amazon.com Advantage account, get yourself an ISDN number (several companies online will do it for you), and send Amazon.com a box of your books.

That's pretty much it. In a couple days, you'll have an Amazon.com listing to share with your friends, family, customers and prospects.

But you aren't writing a book because you suddenly think it's easy. Write a book because it's the ultimate credibility tool. It will quickly make you the expert in your field.

Then, you can use that book as an incentive throughout your business.

Want to drive Web site visitors into your store? Offer them a free copy of your book, just for visiting.

Isn't it often worth a few dollars to meet new customers?

STEP SEVENTY FIVE ACTION ITEMS:
Write a book.

Conclusion

Well, you have some work to do.

But, more importantly, you have money to make.

Prospects to meet.

Customers to make more loyal.

If you've been working as you read, then you have an incredibly diverse, hard-working Web marketing strategy in the field, and likely already producing results.

If you've read through this book first, it's time to go back and read it again. But this time, get to work.

Start at the front, and take it a step at a time. Go as fast or as slow as you want.

This book was written and formatted to help make your Web marketing strategy easier and more comfortable, but it also will likely push you a bit out of your comfort zone.

But that's how we get better. We don't grow by standing pat. We don't keep our competition at bay by doing what we've always done.

My friend, it's time to grow.

Use this book as your starting point, and don't forget to keep learning and innovating.

I'll see you on the Web!

Credits & Copyrights

We hope this book inspires you to innovate your business, and particularly marketing, to achieve the success you've dreamt about. The author was particularly inspired by Seth Godin, Kathy Sierra, John Jantsch, Emerson Robbins, Tom Ferry, John Moore, Ron McDaniel, Richard Nacht, Guy Kawasaki, Jackie Huba, Ben McConnell, Claudia Wicks, Mark Strother, Mark Powell and many many others.

Special thanks to Alan Urdan for his smart design work throughout this book, Maria Geokezas for keeping us on schedule, and to HouseValues for sponsoring this project.

This book is dedicated to my wife, Beth. She knows why.

About the Author

Matt Heinz is Senior Director of Marketing for HouseValues, Inc. (NASDAQ: SOLD), a marketing company providing residential real estate professionals with everything they need to achieve unrivaled success in their business. Matt has more than 10 years of consumer and B-to-B marketing experience with technology, real estate and retail products.

Prior to joining HouseValues, Matt spent five years working for Microsoft (the first three with its PR agency), where he was responsible for driving marketing and business development efforts within the company's MSN unit.

He has previously held marketing positions at The Boeing Company, Weber Shandwick, The Seattle Mariners and the Washington State Attorney General's office.

Matt holds a bachelor's degree from the University of Washington, and lives with his wife and Greater Swiss Mountain Dog in Kirkland, Wash.

Matt's Blog
http://www.mattonmarketing.com

Matt's LinkedIn Profile
http://www.linkedin.com/in/mattheinz